P9-CRS-913

Reading: A Linguistic Perspective

Reading:
A
Linguistic
Perspective

Ronald Wardhaugh
University of Michigan

HARCOURT, BRACE & WORLD, INC.
New York / Chicago / San Francisco / Atlanta

LIBRARY OF CONGRESS CATALOG CARD NUMBER: 71-84055

PRINTED IN THE UNITED STATES OF AMERICA

For Hazel, Bruce, and Carolyn

PREFACE

The possible applications of linguistic knowledge to the teaching of reading have intrigued reading researchers and teachers for some time. There has even been discussion of a "linguistic method" of teaching reading which would focus on the systematic relationships of sounds (phonemes) to letters (graphemes) and the systematic programing of these relationships in beginning reading texts. Linguistics can indeed contribute to the study of reading; what it has to offer, however, is not a method for teaching reading but a body of knowledge about language that reading researchers and teachers can draw on in their work. The material in this book, therefore, provides a *perspective* on the teaching of reading, not a *method* for teaching reading.

While the interest of reading teachers in linguistics has been growing, linguistics itself has been undergoing a revolution. In the last decade, the goals of linguistics and the interests of linguists have changed considerably, but these changes have received almost no attention in the literature on linguistics and reading. *Reading: A Linguistic Perspective* draws on these recent developments, specifically on the work of the generative-transformationalists, and attempts to show how that knowledge may be relevant to the teaching of reading. Of necessity the book is highly tentative, even speculative, in its approach, but given the current state of linguistic theory and knowledge of English, and given the concurrent uncertainties in psychology and pedagogy, it would be rash to attempt a definitive statement about linguistics and reading at this time.

The book therefore draws together some exciting ideas in linguistics and brings them to the attention of reading researchers and teachers. The discussion covers not only English orthography but also syntax, semantics, and dialect, for the contribution that linguistics can make to a better understanding of the teaching of reading involves these topics as well. It assumes some familiarity with the literature on reading and with linguistics, but a glossary of linguistic terms has been included for the reader with little background in linguistics. Concepts from psychology and pedagogy are introduced where they are relevant, in the belief that it would be most unwise either to assume that linguistics can provide all the answers or to ignore valuable contributions from other disciplines. Workers in reading face many problems, some of them linguistic in nature. If, as a result of reading this book, they can confront these problems with fruitful hypotheses based on a growing body of sound information, the book will have achieved its goal.

I would like to express my thanks to the following for suggestions they made during various stages of writing of this book: Harold King, Earl Buxton, Wendell Weaver, Albert Kingston, Kenneth Goodman, Roger Shuy, Julia Gibson, and Robert Krohn. I am particularly indebted to Marcia Heiman for her valuable criticisms of the final manuscript and to Jane Read for her typing of the various versions of the book.

Ronald Wardhaugh

CONTENTS

Reading: A Linguistic Perspective

CHAPTER ONE

The Teaching of Reading

The teaching of reading is unquestionably one of the most important tasks of our schools. It is not the only task, for education is not synonymous with literacy, but literacy is a necessary part of, even a prerequisite to, what modern society regards as a complete education. In an age of mass compulsory education we have undertaken to teach every child to read regardless of almost any handicaps that he might have. We realize too that almost every child comes to school expecting to learn to read within a very short period of time and that his success, or lack of it, in learning to read soon becomes the yardstick by which he judges what goes on in school. Learning to read is the first task he faces in what he knows will be many years of schooling. His first experience with school learning is therefore likely to be critical, particularly since success in subsequent learning tasks will depend heavily on success in that first one.

The child is not alone in judging the school by how successful it is in teaching him to read. Similar judgments are likely to be made by his parents and by the general public. The most damning criticism of any school system is that its products are illiterate. Consequently, school superintendents, principals, and teachers generally choose to defend the success of their work by quoting facts and figures on reading achievement more than any other statistic. Not even new buildings and high teaching salaries seem to exceed reading ability statistics as indicators of the success of a school system. Whenever evidence reveals that particular groups of children are not learning to read successfully, there is almost certain to be widespread public concern leading to the establishment of remedial centers and special programs. Children who still cannot read after several years in school are regarded as educational cripples and apparently regard themselves as such. Since there is a widespread belief that educational cripples are also likely to be or to become social cripples (although the precise causal relationship is not clear), it generally seems wiser for society to invest its economic resources in remedial centers than in reformatories and prisons. Mainly because reading and social failure seem to co-occur those educators most concerned with reading have adopted all-inclusive definitions of it, definitions in which success in reading seems to be equated with success in living. Here, for example, is Gates writing in *The Forty-Eighth Yearbook of The National Society for the Study of Education, Part II*, entitled *Reading in the Elementary School* (1949):

> ... reading is not to be regarded as limited to mental activities. The dynamic and emotional processes are also involved. In wholehearted reading activity the child does more than understand and contemplate; his emotions are stirred; his attitudes and purposes are modified; indeed, his innermost being is involved. That an individual's personality may be deeply affected by his reading is a basic assumption of the emerging practice of bibliotherapy—the treatment of personality maladjustment by means of reading and reflecting upon carefully selected materials. The reading program should, therefore, make provision for exerting an influence upon the development of the most wholesome dynamic and emotional adjustments. (p. 4)

Success in reading is therefore assumed to be closely related to success in living and to personal and emotional adjustment. The successful reader is to some extent also the successful citizen.

In many studies, such as that by Robinson (1946), reading failure is related to one or more of a galaxy of factors such as emotional, social, neurological, psychological, and physiological impairment. Robinson studied thirty cases of reading failure intensively and it is interesting to note her comment about the relationship of teaching methods to reading failure:

Inappropriate school methods accounted for fewer cases of failure than was anticipated, but the full details concerning this factor were difficult to obtain from the group of children studied. (p. 231)

Robinson did not investigate the problems that inappropriate methods might have created for her thirty cases, because she found it difficult to evaluate either the methods or their results. She did say, however, that there apparently was a connection between the teaching methods which were employed and success or failure in reading:

Since a large number of these severely retarded readers improved, it seems logical to assume that better adaptation of methods of teaching reading to some of the deviating cases has greater value than the number of such cases reported in this study indicates. (pp. 226–27)

We cannot minimize the importance of the factors that Robinson chose to emphasize (emotional, social, and so on), but there is questionable validity in the argument that because certain kinds of impairment and reading disability go hand in hand, the second must result from the first. Robinson herself is aware that correlation is not causation, but her caution in interpreting her results has been frequently forgotten.

While there are obvious advantages to be gained from adopting a broad view of both reading and reading disabilities—for example, the advantage of being forced to consider the function of reading in life and in a curriculum designed to make the best of that life—nevertheless dangers abound. The first danger is that a broad view can easily become very superficial. When statements about reading and the purposes of reading are couched in general terms and refer to almost every aspect of life, they tend to become meaningless because they are essentially untestable. If it is not possible to make definitive statements about social adjustment itself, it is no more possible to evaluate statements about the place of the equally ill-defined term *reading* in social adjustment.

A second danger is that every factor that appears to be related to reading tends to be considered equal to every other factor. Eye-movement habits, print size, color blindness, posture, story line, supplementary materials, library resources, sex, teachers' ages, and on and on, all tend to be regarded as equally important. While some factors must obviously be more crucial than others, there is really no way of finding out which ones they are, because they all seem to receive equal attention from reviewers in summaries of research on reading. It should also be noted that these factors multiply faster than systems for handling them, so that we are very far at the moment from an acceptable theory of reading. This situation will continue to exist as long as researchers allow themselves to be side-tracked from the content of reading into its correlates.

A third danger is that when reading becomes synonymous with the whole of education, reading instruction can become the whipping boy for the real or imagined failure of a particular kind of education, as it did for Flesch in his *Why Johnny Can't Read* (1955), with its polemical attack on "progressive" education and the "look-and-say" method of teaching reading. Because Flesch was able to articulate very convincingly many of the prevailing half truths and misgivings about education in general and reading in particular, his criticisms contained just enough credibility to be acceptable to the general public. The reaction of educators to him was quite predictable when they read such statements as:

> Reading means getting meaning from certain combinations of letters. Teach the child what each letter stands for and he can read.
> Ah no, you say, it can't be that simple. But it is. (pp. 2–3)

> Naturally, the stupendous and frighteningly idiotic work of concocting this stuff [series of readers] can only be done by tireless teamwork of many educational drudges. (p. 7)

> Many years ago, when I was about fifteen, I took a semester's course in Czech; I have since forgotten everything about the language itself, but I still remember how the letters are pronounced, plus the simple rule that all words have the accent on the first syllable. Armed with this knowledge, I once surprised a native of Prague by reading aloud from a Czech newspaper. "Oh, you know Czech?" he asked. "No, I don't understand a word of it," I answered. "I can only read it." (p. 23)

Faced with such naive and polemical statements, those under fire closed their ranks against a common enemy, replied to Flesch's obvious oversimplifications and inaccuracies, and ignored valid criticisms he made: the lack of challenge to children in reading texts, the approach to the problems of English spelling which ignored the alphabetical nature of the English writing system, and the procedures used in creating reading series. Actually the criticism voiced by Flesch was not entirely undeserved, because if improved social living is one goal of reading, then failure to achieve such a goal is a reading failure and teachers of reading may legitimately be held responsible for certain kinds of social failure.

Within the discipline of reading itself, controversy over methodology continues. The advantages and disadvantages of various methods of teaching reading, including the "phonics," "look-and-say," and "sentence" methods, have long been under discussion. A basic distinction has been made between methods that emphasize the decoding of print and those that emphasize reading for meaning. The methods themselves have never been closely defined, nor has there been serious examination of exactly what constitutes a method for teaching reading. Each new or revised method has been vigorously proposed and opposed, and each has had its share of blame for causing failure in learning to read and its share of praise for proving effective in remediation. In all this controversy the arguments have not been as well informed as they should have been and have drawn equally freely from fact and myth.

Although the summaries of these controversies by Diack (1965), Mathews (1966), and Chall (1967) are not without their weaknesses and prejudices, they do indicate the general nature of the disagreements over methods. Diack criticizes the reading research on teaching methods on the grounds that it has discovered very little of any consequence; he comes to the conclusion that a satisfactory method for teaching reading would have to be based on a recognition of the alphabetic nature of English and would, to that extent, be a phonics method. Mathews is also critical of reading research on methods; he favors phonics, or the "synthetic plan," as he calls it, because he claims that all the valid research clearly supports that approach:

> The fact is well established that children taught by a carefully worked out synthetic plan read much better and read sooner than those taught by an analytic method, or by any combination of

approaches in which the analytic element predominates. The evidence for this statement is abundant and is constantly being augmented. (p. 196)

Most recently, Chall has come out in favor of a phonics approach in the teaching of beginning reading as a result of her own investigation. All three educators show clearly that the nature of the controversies over methodology has not changed much over the years and that while the quantity of evidence supporting or refuting a particular method has increased quite rapidly, the quality of that evidence remains very poor indeed. In such circumstances it is not surprising that the results of reading investigations are often inconclusive or contradictory. Since the investigations are usually made by protagonists or antagonists of a particular method, working within a system in which there is a great weight of "conventional wisdom" and a marked resistance to any but very slow change, it is understandable that any research, good or bad, tends to be ineffectual in promoting change.

Chall has pointed out that reading research has been characterized by ill-defined terms and goals, by the Hawthorne or halo effects of experimentation, by the non-cumulative "one shot" attack on problems, by contrary interpretations of data, and by unwarranted conclusions. While much of this criticism is merited, some advances in knowledge have been gained, and reading research is not entirely a wasteland. It is still easy to agree with Carroll's observation (1964a), however, that "much of the research on reading, even when methodologically sound, has been of little use because the teaching procedures examined by the research were not thoroughly sound." (p. 351) And, of course, basic to the particular teaching procedures examined has been the view of language on which each procedure was based. Generally that view has been at least a generation behind current knowledge.

One of the clearest ways of showing some of the inadequacies of research and knowledge in reading is to look closely at a single aspect of current reading instruction, that aspect called phonics. A great deal of what has been written on the subject of phonics is inaccurate when it is judged against what we know today about language. This last remark should not, of course, be construed as an attack on phonics itself as a way of teaching children to understand the relationship between letters and sounds, and of providing them with the skills necessary to approach written words they have not previously encountered. It is rather a criticism of the way in which phonics is sometimes presented in texts and articles on reading, because such materials often contain false and misleading statements about language. For example, English is sometimes said to be an "un-phonetic" language or "one of the least phonetically lawful" languages. This is obviously not so, because every natural language is phonetic in that it makes use of sound. It is true that English does not seem to be spelled as consistently as it could be, but that fact has nothing to do with its phonetic nature. Phonetics is that branch of linguistic science which is concerned with how sounds may be produced, analyzed, and recorded in all their possible variety and, as a discipline, has nothing to do with spelling systems as such. Phonetic knowledge of a language is, of course, invaluable to anyone who wishes to devise an orthography for a language, but it is only one of several kinds of knowledge which must be brought to bear on that problem. The language itself is quite independent of the particular orthography that is used to represent it. It is no less phonetic if that orthography is a poor one or if it is syllabic or logographic rather than alphabetic. The term *phonetics* refers to sounds, and should not be lightly used to refer to the regularity or irregularity of sound-symbol relationships. Misuse of the term is likely to result in the confused thinking and writing all too prevalent in the literature on phonics and reading instruction.

English is sometimes said to have five vowels (or six or seven). Again such a statement is inaccurate, because the number of vowel contrasts in the surface phonology of English—that is, in minimal pairs of words such as *bit* and *beat* or *cap* and *cup*—is generally at least twice that number for any speaker of the language. This is a further instance of obvious confusion between a statement about the sounds of English and a statement about the letters and combinations of letters that represent those sounds. More than a century and a half ago Sir William Jones criticized those who claimed that English had five vowels. Only recently have such criticisms been heeded as some of the concepts of the linguist have been introduced into the literature on reading. The result has been a welcome loss of innocence and a much more serious approach to understanding exactly what vowels are, how they differ, and how they are represented in the orthography.

To take another example, English vowels are often described as being "long" or "short." The long ones are sometimes said to "say their own names." In actual fact the vowel in *beat* is shorter in duration than the vowel in *jazz.* English vowels do not contrast with each other in duration. It is true that some vowels are longer in duration than others, but such differences are not *significant*—that is, they never result in a difference in meaning in English. In linguistic terms, they are *allophonic differences,* differences in the effect of specific environments. Thus it is automatically a fact of English that a vowel before a voiceless consonant, such as *p, t, k, f,* or *s,* is shorter in duration than the same vowel before a corresponding voiced consonant, such as *b, d, g, v,* or *z,* and that a final vowel—that is, a vowel at the end of a word—is longer than either. A native speaker of English can demonstrate these facts for himself by repeating *beat, bead, bee* or *loop, lube, Lou* or *place, plays, play.* Vowels such as those in *bit* and *cup* also show the same duration variations: the vowel in *bit* is shorter in duration than the one in *bid* and the vowel in *cup* is shorter in duration than the one in *cub.* These vowels, of course, do not occur in final position. The important term in discussing length or duration of vowels is *significant.* Only significant differences are important in a linguistic system. Non-significant differences are by definition unimportant, because native speakers never use non-significant differences to distinguish one utterance from another. Clearly the notion of significance is an important one which cannot be ignored in a discussion of English phonology. Nor should it be ignored in any method of teaching reading that relies heavily on an accurate knowledge of that phonology.

Discussions of phonics methods frequently describe *th, sh, qu,* and *wh* variously as digraphs ("two letters combining to produce a new sound") or blends ("two letters blending their sounds together"); again such descriptions are mixtures of fact and fiction. *Th,* whether the *th* of *then* or *thin,* and *sh* as in *ship,* represent unitary sounds in English—that is, single phonemes—whereas *qu,* as in *quick,* represents two sounds [kw], a sequence of phonemes. *Wh,* as in *which,* also represents two sounds, but only in those dialects where there is a genuine phonological contrast between *which* and *witch*. Many millions of speakers of English make no contrast between these last two words but pronounce both as [wɪč]. These speakers do not confuse the two words because the words are quite differently distributed grammatically. In those dialects where there is a contrast, it is of very limited importance—nothing like the importance of the *bit-pit* contrast, for example. Teaching children to make a contrast between [hw] and [w] when they do not make the contrast in their dialect seems to be little more than wasted effort in such circumstances.

Another feature of phonics is a great emphasis on rules for syllabication. Reading teachers are asked to teach their children to divide words as follows: *but-ter, mon-key, rob-in, ro-bot,* even though, as has been pointed out elsewhere (Wardhaugh, 1966), such rules are often quite circular, have almost nothing to do with the actual sound patterns of English and almost everything to do with line-breaking conventions, and have hardly any possible application beyond the typesetter's domain. They certainly do not make sense as a systematic statement about the syllables of the spoken language, nor are they entirely consistent with one another. The "rules for syllabication" are extremely complicated, in fact so complicated that if children can use them, they do not really need them, because their use requires that children have the very knowledge the rules are supposed to be teaching. On the other hand, statements about units such as prefixes, roots, and suffixes and for compounding do have some value.

An examination of almost any writing on phonics will reveal examples of misconception such as these. All too frequently we encounter statements such as the following:

> Consonant blends consist of two or more letters which are blended into a single speech sound. (Heilman, 1964, p. 31)

> The [five- or six-year-old] child has not mastered the sophisticated knowledge of speech sounds that the linguist's statement [that the preschool child is able to discriminate the letter sounds (*sic*) in words] implies. To the child, the spoken equivalent of *cat* is a unitary or global sound which he can differentiate globally from all other language units called words. (Heilman, 1964, p. 11)

Letters do not blend to make sounds; five- and six-year-olds are able to speak so must control the sound system of the language; and children can differentiate *cat* from *rat, fat, mat, sat, pat,* and so on, so must be reacting to some sound unit smaller than the "global" one mentioned by Heilman.

Confused ideas about the relationship of speech to writing, language variation, phonological systems, and the linguistic abilities of children are handed on to generations of reading teachers. Only recently have some books appeared which reveal more linguistic sophistication; Durkin's *Phonics and the Teaching of Reading* (1965) is possibly the best of these.

A series of articles in *The Reading Teacher* has reported on the usefulness of phonic generalizations. These articles by Clymer (1963), Bailey (1967), Emans (1967), and Burmeister (1968) are based on studies in which a number of basic phonic generalizations were examined for their utility when applied to words in various texts. No attempt was made to examine the generalizations themselves for their linguistic sense or to order them in any way. The only criterion was their usefulness, not their soundness. For example, each of the following generalizations was accepted at face value:

"In many two- and three-syllable words, the final *e* lengthens the vowel in the last syllable."

"If the last syllable of a word ends in *le,* the consonant preceding the *le* usually begins the last syllable."

"In *ay* the *y* is silent and gives *a* its long sound."

Moreover, some of the generalizations obviously require ordering, so that a generalization such as "The *r* gives the preceding vowel a sound that is neither long nor short" must precede one that says "When a vowel is in the middle of a one-syllable word, the vowel is short." The second generalization therefore would not be applied to monosyllabic words containing an *r* after a single vowel letter because such words would already have been covered through application of the first generalization. The generalizations seem to be a haphazard set in which rules about accent, word-splitting, silent letters, and special combinations are presented randomly. Burmeister's conclusion that not many of them are very useful is hardly surprising, because it is hard to imagine that a child could ever learn to read by applying a set of rules of this kind. A more fruitful approach would be to evaluate each generalization, order the valid ones, and examine the texts in the light of this smaller ordered set.

Many of the same criticisms can be leveled against the other methods of teaching reading. The "look-and-say" or "global" method recognizes that meaning is important and that English words are often irregularly spelled; the "sentence" method treats the sentence as the unit of thought and emphasizes the child's experience as the key to his success in learning to read. Thus both methods stress certain aspects of language. But both are obviously inadequate by themselves, for the reasons that repetition does not guarantee learning, that words are not language in any significant sense, and that sentences can assume such a diversity that to rely on sentences produced at random by children for the content of a reading program is to have in reality no program at all. Again, research into word frequency, sentence types, spelling irregularities, and so on has been prolific but often misguided or out-of-date before even begun. Before an investigator counts or computes something, whether it is syllables per word, word frequencies, noun-verb ratios, or sentence patterns, he should have a good idea of what it is that he is counting and some theoretical justification for choosing one set of items to count rather than another. What are syllables, nouns, clauses, and sentences, if these units are the ones the investigator chooses? How does he define them and on what basis does he justify his definitions? Linguists find it extremely difficult to define *syllable, word,* and *sentence* for English, so we may well ask how trustworthy is the "research evidence" on these matters to which reading experts appeal.

Not all reading research is misdirected, and not all of it is unusable; there are obviously valid findings in some of the psychological, physiological, and pedagogical research studies. But the more valid the study, the less closely it seems to be connected with the content of reading and the more closely with child development or social adjustment. The best teaching of reading—that is, reading as it concerns itself with getting meaning from the printed page—seems to be based not so much on research findings but on experience. The good reading teacher seems to have learned what to do and what not to do by teaching reading, not by digesting research studies. Both Fries (1963) and Diack (1965) have made just this point. After an extensive review of the literature on reading research, Fries concluded:

> *I have not been able to find the evidence to justify the assertion that the published findings of recent educational research [since 1916] have provided the basis of most of the modern reforms in reading instruction.* (p. 29)

After a similar inspection of the research literature, Diack's conclusion is almost the same:

> Perhaps I am giving the impression that research into reading during the past fifty years has been singularly unprofitable. This is an impression I am reluctant to give, but there is very little I can do about it, for in some years of reading on this subject I came across nothing in the way of research which I felt showed something that a mixture of keen observation and shrewd common sense could not have found out—except perhaps the clever photography of Buswell and a few others which produced much more accurate records of eye-movements in reading than had existed before. (p. 179)

What seems called for in reading is a focus on a somewhat narrower view. For a while, at least, it would be well to return to a basic concern with reading as it relates to language, so that a more rigorous examination can be made of such relationships as sounds to letters, words to meanings, sentences to sense, and so on. One can hope that as a result investigators will find a few genuine causes for reading disability and that they will prefer to do this rather than to study a bewildering multiplicity of symptoms.

A linguistic perspective on reading may result in more rigorous and meaningful research and in the end more effective methods of teaching reading. The word *perspective* rather than *method* is deliberately chosen. There can be no linguistic method or methods in teaching reading. There may well be many different methods that can be used in the teaching of reading, but linguistics as a discipline offers no method for such teaching, just as it offers no methods for teaching first or second languages, or probably anything else. Linguistics is a way of studying language and is essentially a "pure" discipline—that is, pure in the sense of theoretical, like theoretical physics or theoretical chemistry. Applied linguistics draws on the pure study but also demands an understanding of many other kinds of knowledge, just as engineering draws on other disciplines besides physics. Methods and techniques for pursuing theoretical studies in linguistics are not necessarily appropriate to applied studies, but unfortunately the opposite assumption has often been made, sometimes by linguists and at other times by those who want to use linguistic findings directly and immediately. Linguistics does, however, offer important insights into many problems that confront the reading teacher and reading researcher. To that extent it offers each a perspective from which he can profitably view the various tasks he faces in teaching reading, in experimenting with different methods and techniques, and in devising remedial programs.

CHAPTER TWO

Recent Proposals on Linguistics and Reading

In recent years several proposals have been made for integrating linguistic findings into the teaching of reading, and annual meetings of the International Reading Association and of other groups of educators have featured sectional meetings and workshops devoted to topics such as "The Role of Linguistics," "Psycholinguistics and Reading Instruction," "Research in Linguistics and Reading Instruction," and "Linguistic Principles and Reading Practices." The idea is abroad that there is a *linguistic* method of teaching reading that is somehow different from a *phonics* method or a *look-and-say* method or from any other method. There are also various reading series available for classroom use which are advertised as linguistic in either content or approach, or in some other way are proclaimed as having some kind of "linguistic" content in that they are "phonological linguistic" or "phonemically based" or "spelling patterned." Once again it must be emphasized that there can be no such method as a linguistic method of teaching reading. Although it is possible to make various proposals for using the findings of linguistic research in the teaching of reading, *these proposals by no means add up to a method of teaching reading.* An adequate method of teaching reading must draw on insights from many other disciplines in addition to linguistics. Linguists are but one group which may have a legitimate interest in the teaching of reading.

The earliest proposals to use modern linguistic knowledge in the teaching of reading came from Leonard Bloomfield, professor of linguistics at Yale for many years and one of the founders of modern American linguistics. Bloomfield was disturbed by the kind of instruction being offered in the schools of his time, particularly that in language and in reading. In fact, in a statement published in the very first volume of *Language* explaining why the Linguistic Society of America had been founded, he gave the following as one of the reasons (Bloomfield, 1925):

> Our schools are conducted by persons who, from professors of education down to teachers in the classroom, know nothing of the results of linguistic science, not even the relation of writing to speech or of standard language to dialect. In short, they do not know what language is, and yet must teach it, and in consequence waste years of every child's life and reach a poor result. (p. 5)

Bloomfield was particularly critical of the instruction in reading given to his son, because he felt that the methods employed were unscientific and revealed a lack of awareness of the discoveries of linguistic science. He therefore devised his own method of teaching his son to read and shared his opinions, his methods, and his materials with those of his friends who were also interested in this problem. These later became known as the Bloomfield system for teaching reading when they found their way into *Let's Read* (Bloomfield and Barnhart, 1961).

Bloomfield rejected traditional phonics as a way of teaching reading, because he said that the proponents of phonics confused speech and writing and often thought that they were teaching the child to speak whereas all they were really doing was teaching the child to associate written symbols with words he already knew. He also objected to the fact that teachers who used phonic methods broke up words into smaller parts corresponding to letters and talked about the sounds associated with individual letters. Bloomfield insisted that such sounds could not properly be isolated: he felt that for example, *put* is a unit which cannot be broken down and sounded out as [pʻə], [ʊ], and [tʻə]. He was adamantly opposed to any notions of sounding out words and of blending sounds in an attempt to decode written words. To Bloomfield, words were complete units which could not be broken down in such a way. On the other hand, Bloomfield did not favor what is sometimes referred to as whole-word approach or method. The whole-word method, claimed Bloomfield, ignores the alphabetic nature of English and treats it as though it were Chinese. Any method which tries to go straight from the written symbol to meaning also ignores the facts that writing is a representation of speech and that there is a necessary mediating level of speech in the process, although this may not be overt. Just as there was to be no sounding out, there was also to be no early emphasis on silent reading, on going straight from the written symbol to meaning without going through the mediating stage of oral reading.

In the initial stage of teaching reading, Bloomfield required that children be trained in visual discrimination and then be taught to associate visually discriminated objects—that is, letter and word shapes—to already known sounds and meanings. He thought that the story line and meaning of reading materials were far less important than the regularity of the connections between sounds and symbols—that is, of the phoneme-grapheme correspondences. In order to guarantee that children should easily acquire a mastery of these correspondences, Bloomfield insisted that they be trained to discriminate in a left-to-right direction and also to name the letters of the alphabet without error. He believed that requiring children to name the letters in new words from left to right guaranteed both visual discrimination and correct word attack. The naming of letters had no other function in Bloomfield's method than this one of insuring discrimination. It had nothing to do with sounding out, nor with the well-known finding that children who know the alphabet when they come to school generally experience little difficulty in learning to read. Bloomfield did not confuse correlation with causation. He always insisted that words be pronounced as wholes and never letter by letter, so that although his method required children to say that *cat* is spelled *c, a,* and *t,* they would never attempt to pronounce it as anything but [kæt]. The Bloomfield approach is therefore not phonics as it has usually been conceived, and Flesch was quite wrong to place Bloomfield alongside those proponents of phonics methods who were his contemporaries. It is phonics only in that the words to be presented to children would show a regularity of sound-symbol, or phoneme-grapheme, correspondence and that there would be only one symbol for each sound until children came to realize that writing is a representation of speech and on the whole quite a systematic one.

Bloomfield was very critical of phonics as it was usually taught, because he felt that teachers confused writing with speech, confused the teaching of reading with teaching children to speak, and confused children by attempting to isolate sounds and by stressing phonetic details that were either irrelevant or plainly misleading. He saw a need to teach written words such as *can, van,* and *fan* in contrast with each other and also to introduce all the contrastive details of the English writing system gradually and systematically, so that the child learning to read would realize that "printed letter= speech sound to be spoken" (Bloomfield and Barnhart, 1961, p. 36). It is not surprising that the resulting lists and exercises look not a little like the old "word family" lists in many older readers.

Believing that the major task in initial reading is wholly concerned with the interpretation of words and not with guessing at their meanings by using accompanying illustrations, Bloomfield also rejected pictures in readers as being either irrelevant or misleading. This idea that beginning reading texts should not have illustrations has appealed to linguists other than Bloomfield. Hall (1964), for example, has written:

> A satisfactory elementary reading text should never have pictures or illustrations of any kind; on the other hand, special devices for emphasizing irregularities (e.g., special colors for silent letters or for those used in unusual values) might well be incorporated, at least in the initial stages. (p. 432)

Some of the materials that Fries and his followers were to develop following Bloomfield's example also contain no pictures, so that children may be left free to focus their attention on the reading materials themselves.

Since, according to Bloomfield, the basic task the child had to master was the task of understanding the spelling system of English and not the meanings of English words and sentences, nonsense syllables and nonsense words could profitably be used in achieving such mastery, and both are employed in texts and tests. Bloomfield advised on their use:

> Tell the child that the nonsense syllables are parts of real words which he will find in the books that he reads. For example, the child will know *han* in *handle* and *jan* in *January* and *mag* in *magnet* or *magpie*. The acquisition of nonsense syllables is an important part of the task of mastering the reading process. The child will learn the patterns of the language more rapidly if you use the nonsense syllables in teaching. (Bloomfield and Barnhart, 1961, pp. 41–42)

Later another linguist, Hall (1964), was to give similar advice about nonsense syllables:

> The ultimate test of any method of teaching reading is whether the learners can deal with nonsense-syllables; if a child cannot read off *glump, trib,* or *donk,* not caring whether these syllables have a real-life meaning or not, the method has failed. (p. 432)

All this advice is somewhat reminiscent of the moribund technique of "finding little words in big words!" It should be noted too that Bloomfield was concerned on the whole with monosyllabic words, and that polysyllabic words received very little attention. In defense of this emphasis, Bloomfield claimed that his son found no difficulty in transferring to polysyllabic words once he had achieved a mastery of the monosyllabic patterns.

Bloomfield also recognized that children who come to school know the language and that it is the task of the school to teach reading, not speaking, to teach a new and different codification of a system that children already possess and to do it systematically. Five- and six-year-old children use their language easily, unconsciously, and essentially grammatically. It is the school's task to draw on the knowledge that children bring to school in any program designed to teach them to read. Such a program need not be concerned with teaching children about their language, or teaching them new words, or new meanings for words, or a new dialect. In beginning reading the task is to teach children to break a new code and not to teach them new messages.

There is much that is admirable in Bloomfield's ideas about reading. First of all, his work on English phoneme-grapheme correspondences was based on a developing knowledge of the important phonological contrasts of English. Today there exist other views of English phonology than the one found in Bloomfield's work, but Bloomfield's statements are no less important for that reason. Further, Bloomfield stressed that English spelling is basically alphabetical and not as inconsistent as it is often made out to be, particularly when it is approached from the viewpoint of how sounds are represented in writing and not how letters are pronounced. Then, too, there is in his work a welcome insistence that the proper content of reading is basically to be found in language rather than in social and psychological factors. Unfortunately, Bloomfield's work appeared at a time when ideas very different from his were strongly entrenched in education. Consequently he was unable to find a publisher during his lifetime, and only Barnhart's efforts resulted in publication of the work after Bloomfield's death. Bloomfield's insistence on a concern with the fundamentals of reading instruction was therefore overlooked, misinterpreted, or ignored by educators whose concerns were with such matters as social adjustment and all-round development. Only later did it become obvious that such general goals could not be achieved without an insistence on certain fundamentals, because good social adjustment could not regularly be achieved by non-readers and practices which ignored these fundamentals apparently turned out too many non-readers.

The Bloomfield system has many advocates and has profoundly influenced the writings of several other people on linguistics and reading, notably Charles Fries. While the Bloomfield system has much to recommend it, it also has very definite weaknesses. There is perhaps too much emphasis on phonemic-graphemic regularities and on word recognition and not enough acknowledgment that some inconsistently spelled English words must be introduced very early in reading texts in order to make reading materials interesting from the beginning. Sometimes the method has been modified to introduce a minimum of "sight words" so that stories can be made more interesting. Such modifications have never appeared to be very important ones, because Bloomfield and his followers considered that the intrinsic reward of being able to read would tend to compensate a child for any lack of interest the material might have. Actually, the Bloomfield method has much more to say about the linguistic content of reading materials than about any method of teaching reading. What comments on methodology there are in Bloomfield's writings seem to be based on an extrapolation of some procedures, such as contrast, which linguists have found useful in their work, and not on procedures derived from teaching reading. Soffietti (1955) quotes Bloomfield's writings extensively in setting out a linguistically based approach to reading instruction. In particular he emphasizes that the meaning of a passage is not triggered directly by the visual stimuli of writing; he claims that it is necessary for the reader to go through an intermediate stage in which the visual stimuli are either vocalized or subvocalized. These vocalizations or subvocalizations in turn release the meanings of the written words. Soffietti adds:

> Obviously, reading will be an easy or difficult skill to learn, depending on the ease or difficulty encountered by the individual in the perception and vocalization of the written forms, i.e., in recognizing what sounds the written forms are meant to spell. (p. 70)

The total program Soffietti recommends is much like Bloomfield's, particularly in his insistence on the importance of introducing consistent spelling representations for individual sounds and of omitting irregularly spelled words until the basic alphabetic principle of English has been presented thoroughly in beginning reading texts. He is of the opinion too that reading experts have tended to concentrate on meaning and the problems of getting meaning directly from the printed page at the expense of achieving an adequate understanding of the reading program, and particularly of the critical importance of sound-symbol relationships in that process. In one way Soffietti goes further than Bloomfield in that he advocates an early introduction of the skills of written communication in an ordered approach.

A more recent proposal to use linguistics in reading, and almost certainly an improvement over both Bloomfield's and Soffietti's, was made by Fries in his book *Linguistics and Reading* (1963). Like Bloomfield, Fries was a leading figure in American linguistics, achieving distinction for his work in English linguistics and in the application of linguistics to teaching English as a foreign language. With his interest in applied linguistics, it is not surprising that he should have turned his attention to reading and that he should have published what undoubtedly is the most influential book on linguistics and reading to date. Fries' interest in the teaching of reading grew in part out of teaching young children to read and was nurtured by discussions with Bloomfield and others of the problems involved. The book is the product of two decades spent considering such problems, and a lifetime of work in English and linguistics. Fries took the position that reading experts are quite unfamiliar with linguistics and in general exhibit little knowledge of language at all; consequently, he set out to correct this defect and to offer an outline of a reading method that would draw heavily on linguistic insights. He criticized the unscholarliness of research in reading methodology in general and disputed the claim that research in reading has made a noticeable contribution to the better teaching of reading in the twentieth century.

One important distinction that Fries insisted on is in the use of the terms *phonics, phonetics,* and *phonemics;* a chapter of his book is devoted to clarifying the differences among these terms and setting the record straight. The chapter contains example after example of the confused use of the three terms in the literature on reading and is a rather telling indictment of most writing on the subject of phonics. Fries defined the three terms clearly as follows:

Phonics has been and continues to be a way of teaching beginning reading. It consists primarily in attempting to match the individual letters by which a word is spelled with the specific "sounds" which these letters "say." *Phonics* is used by some teachers as one of the methods of helping pupils, who have acquired a "sight-vocabulary" of approximately 200 words, to solve the problems presented by "new" words by "sounding" the letters.

Phonetics is *not* the same set of materials and activities as *phonics.* *Phonetics* is a set of techniques by which to identify and describe, in absolute terms, all the differences of sound features that occur in any language. *Phonetics* is not concerned with the ways in which words are spelled in English by the traditional alphabet. "Phonetic" alphabets have been constructed to serve as tools to represent graphically the actual pronunciations of linguistic forms, and these alphabets have been tried from time to time in the efforts to achieve a more effective way of teaching beginning reading.

Phonemics is a set of techniques by which to identify and to describe, especially in terms of distribution, the bundles of sound contrasts that constitute the structural units that mark the word-patterns. It is the *phonemes* of the language that alphabetic writing represents. (p. 156)

Fries emphasized the point that written English is alphabetic in nature and that English spelling is not as inconsistent as it is said to be, if statements about speech and statements about writing are clearly distinguished and if spellings are regarded as representations of significant speech sounds. He insisted that there are regular spelling patterns in English, and it is the reading teacher's task to teach these patterns from the beginning by presenting them in carefully arranged sequences and giving beginning readers considerable practice in recognizing them, particularly in contrast to each other within monosyllabic words.

Fries considered that reading was a new visual task for children. They had to learn to associate visual responses with previously discriminated auditory responses and to make these visual responses at high speed, even automatically. Fries believed that this "transfer" process required visual training, such as training in left-to-right eye movements and in the discrimination of the important features of letters and words. For this reason he rejected the introduction of both upper and lower case letters at the same time in beginning texts in favor of the exclusive use of upper case letters, so that the burden of discrimination would be reduced for the child who was learning to read. He apparently rejected the argument that elimination of ascenders and descenders and the resultant uniform "block" shapes of written words would result in the loss of many useful visual clues. Instead he believed that children would find written words composed out of twenty-six uniform letters easier to perceive than the corresponding words composed out of twice that number of letters.

Fries also insisted on the use of contrastive word patterns, because he considered the principle of contrast basic to both linguistic structure and visual perception. He rejected the spelling out of words that Bloomfield recommended, insisting instead that what is critically important for children is to be able to make visual discriminations between whole words and between whole patterns or units of meaning. He sought, therefore, to minimize any factor that would tend to require children to focus on units smaller than whole words.

Although English is alphabetic and the alphabet itself is a contrastive system, Fries believed that the more important system of contrasts was the one associated with words and meanings; consequently, his method was essentially a "word" method. Fries also stressed the importance of oral reading, in the belief that the written message is but a representation of the oral message; the goal, however, was still silent sight reading in the later stages of the program. The content—that is, the story line—took on importance for Fries as his program developed, as did a few of the common sight words, those irregularly spelled words without which it is impossible to write at any length and with any great interest.

Like both Bloomfield and Hall, Fries had very little to say about comprehension: all three writers appear to regard comprehension as a basically passive activity or an activity highly dependent on oral language skills. Children must learn to react instantly to the contrast between *mat* and *mate* and that between *bit* and *beat*. They already react to the differences between these words when they are spoken, and what they must do in learning to read is to associate a visual pattern which they have learned to discriminate from other visual patterns to a speech pattern which they already know and can discriminate from other speech patterns. Fries insisted that meaning is gained through an awareness of structure. He denied that he was not interested in meaning, pointing out that on the contrary, as a linguist, he was concerned with various kinds of meanings. In a letter to Chall, Fries wrote as follows:

> Our approach is certainly *not* a phonic approach. It is *not* an approach that gives primary emphasis to decoding. . . . We should have to insist that our type of approach gives primary emphasis to *reading* for *meanings*.
>
> Notice also that we have said 'reading for meanings' for we are concerned from the very beginning with not only situation meanings but with the lexical meanings of the words, the structural meanings of the sentences, and the cumulative meanings of the succession of sentences as connected by sequence signals into a unit. . . . (Chall, 1967, p. 343)

A child learning to read is already subconsciously aware of the different kinds of meaning in his language, or he could not communicate in that language. What he needs to have unlocked for him is the spelling system so that he can have access to these different kinds of meaning through the medium of print. Fries went so far as to claim that this system, or code, can be unlocked for the beginning reader within a year of his learning to "talk satisfactorily," an age which he put at four or five. The problem of teaching reading comprehension, then, was not a serious one for Fries. He obviously took issue with wide-ranging definitions of the reading process in favor of a view that reading is a kind of high-speed recognition of meanings already familiar to the reader. Reading comprehension is therefore a specific instance of general linguistic comprehension.

The materials written by Fries and his co-workers have concentrated on the beginning reading stages and are not really designed for use in the later stages. If the point of view expressed by Fries is correct, however, there need be little or no concern with teaching reading in the later stages, because all the problems should have been overcome by good initial teaching. In Fries' book *Linguistics and Reading* only four and seven pages respectively are devoted to the two later stages of reading instruction, the *productive* stage, in which the reader "seems to respond to the meanings that are signalled without the use of the signals themselves" (p. 205), and the *imaginative* stage, in which "reading . . . stimulates a vivid imaginative realization of vicarious experience." (p. 208)

In both the Bloomfield and Fries approaches there is a strong insistence that a particular kind of linguistic knowledge is of paramount importance in determining the content of a reading series and an assumption that principles of linguistic analysis such as patterning and contrast can by extrapolation become useful principles in reading pedagogy. Another linguist, Henry Lee Smith, in a review of *Let's Read* (1963), has pointed out that there are certain valid pedagogical principles that linguists have tended to ignore when they have talked about reading. He points out that such matters as typography and layout need to be considered, that pictures may be found to be useful to illustrate stories rather than to tell them, that a certain amount of repetition of patterns and words is very necessary, and that both story line and characters are extremely important. He cautions that it would be unwise for linguists who take an interest in reading to assume that reading teachers have learned nothing from their experiences, either individually or collectively, and he adds that many non-linguistic factors are important, naming such examples as the findings of learning psychology and the principles of gradation. Smith's words have been heeded to some extent in recent writings on linguistics and reading. They were obviously motivated in part by the hostility that characterized the original linguistics-reading discussions. That such hostility, particularly on the part of the reading experts, should have been created is not surprising when one reads some of the statements made by linguists about reading. For example, the statements by Fries and Hall that there should be no illustrations in reading texts and that reading is a passive skill run counter to what most authorities on reading consider to be pedagogically sound observations. It should be emphasized that linguistics as a discipline has nothing at all to contribute to the discussion of whether or not there should be illustrations in a reading text; the inclusion or exclusion of illustrations is entirely a pedagogical decision. Likewise, any definition of reading which makes it out to be a passive skill reveals the author of the definition as having only a superficial awareness of the many problems inherent in the teaching of reading.

It would not be unfair to say that what has become known as the linguistic method of teaching reading relies heavily on the work of Bloomfield and Fries. In essence, the method entails little more than the presentation of regular phoneme-grapheme, or sound-spelling, relationships in beginning reading texts, a kind of new phonics with a good, undoubtedly much needed, dose of linguistic common sense added. The materials developed by the followers of Bloomfield and Fries reflect this concern, and they contain virtually no indication that the possible linguistic contribution to reading involves anything more than the systematic introduction of the regularities and irregularities of English spelling. There is, in fact, scarcely more than an occasional passing reference to any other point that linguists have made about English.

Perhaps the linguistic innovation that has met with most acceptance from workers in reading has been the Initial Teaching Alphabet (previously the Augmented Roman Alphabet) or *i.t.a.* It is a linguistic innovation only insofar as it is concerned with the regularizing of English phoneme-grapheme correspondences through the use of a modified alphabet for beginning reading texts. As recounted by Harrison (1964), this alphabet devised by Sir James Pitman arose out of the failure of the spelling reform movement, the move-

ment that sought a complete reform of English spelling along phonemic principles. After the failure of the spelling reform movement
some of the leaders in the movement turned to the much more
limited goal of reforming or regularizing English spelling for a
specific purpose only, that purpose being the teaching of beginning
reading.

The version of the alphabet in use today makes use of only one
set of 44 characters based on the lower case letters of traditional
orthography but uses these characters in two different sizes—a
smaller size for the traditional lower case letter distribution and a
larger size for the traditional upper case letter distribution. The
design of the type face preserves almost intact the shape of the top
half of each traditional letter that is used. Studies of efficient readers
have indicated that they depend more on the upper parts of letter
shapes for letter and word recognition than on the lower parts;
consequently Pitman felt that preserving the upper parts would lead
to an easier transition to *t.o.* (traditional orthography). The problem
associated with the spelling of the "long" vowels is met by changing
basic letter ordering so that, for example, *mine* becomes *mien,* with
the *i* and *e* run together as *ie.* The phonemic basis of *i.t.a.* is shown
in the difference between the endings of *spelliŋz* and *alfabets* where
the voiced and voiceless sibilants are shown to contrast in the different characters but not to the extent that *sip* and *zip* contrast.
The alphabet contrasts *z* and *s* in the first case but *z* and *s* in the
second. There are many departures from the phonemic principle:
for example, all the traditional double letters are preserved and no
use is made of the schwa symbol [ə]. Anyone trying to write pub-
lishable material in *i.t.a.* requires a manual such as McBride's
Teachers' Course in Writing in i.t.a. (1965) in order to be successful,
because many of the rules for transcription turn out to be quite *ad
hoc,* for example *serv, girl,* and *curl* but *wurd* and *erþ; muʧ* but
matʧ; bridʒ but *sœldier;* and so on. The Initial Teaching Alphabet
is, then, an amalgam of linguistic, perceptual, pedagogical, and
intuitive knowledge. There is no need for the individual teacher and
student to follow all the principles outlined by McBride, because
the devisers of the orthography want it to be adaptable to a variety
of dialects and to serve each user as a temporary expedient only.
For more permanent materials written in *i.t.a.* Harrison quotes the
following estimates (p. 114) of modifications of traditional spellings:

26.5% of words are unchanged *(given, and)*; 23.75% show minor modifications *(rich, is)*; 10.5% show similar forms with no change in movement *(hav, tiem)*; and 39.25% show radical changes *(cof, wuns)*.

In recent years considerable interest has been shown in *i.t.a.* in both England and North America. Since *i.t.a.* can be used with any kind of teaching method, it cuts completely across traditional preferences for one method against another. It also looks sufficiently like traditional orthography to avoid the worst excesses of some of the other modified orthographies that have been proposed for English. The results of most of the experiments with *i.t.a.* that have been reported so far are on the whole favorable, but such results are not wholly unexpected given the experimental conditions. In a review of the experimental work on the effects of *i.t.a.*, Southgate (1966) has pointed out how the conditions behind the experiments have led to considerable Hawthorne effects which undoubtedly have influenced those results. In spite of the lack of conclusive evidence for the success of *i.t.a.*, it still seems that a good case can be made out for regularizing English spelling in some way, at least for the purposes of teaching beginning reading. Perhaps the lesson to be learned from experiences with *i.t.a.* is that anyone who makes such a regularization must bring to the task information from a variety of sources.

The most recent attempt to show the relevance of linguistics to reading is that by Lefevre in his book *Linguistics and the Teaching of Reading* (1964). The book actually contains considerably more material on structural linguistics than on the connection between linguistics and reading, but this emphasis is apparently intentional, a kind of counter to what Lefevre obviously considers to be the conspicuous lack of awareness of linguistic knowledge by reading experts and reading teachers. Lefevre is also concerned with a much broader view of linguistic knowledge than was either Bloomfield or Fries. He points out that it is not enough to consider only phonemic-graphemic correspondences and the ordering of difficulties of spelling patterns in applying linguistic insights to the teaching of reading. His concern is with structures and patterns, particularly sentence patterns, and with the fact that children learning to read must learn to make the visual patterns presented to them correspond with the spoken patterns with which they are already familiar. Lefevre therefore sets out a whole sentence approach, "a new sentence method of teaching reading" (p. xviii), since he considers the sentence to be the critical linguistic unit in reading.

Lefevre is severely critical of reading teachers and researchers who regard the word as the basic unit of language and reading. He is also severely critical of Bloomfield and only a little less so of Fries for the same reason, since the methods they advocate are restricted to the word level. He points out that the word is not the most important unit in language or in reading, that words achieve meaning from their contexts, and that to teach children to recognize words in lists is merely to practice a kind of "word calling." Lefevre insists that the sentence is the unit with which reading teachers should be concerned. Sentences are patterned, and it is sentence patterns that contrast with each other, not word patterns. Words combine into patterns, and it is the patterns that convey meanings. An adequate method for teaching reading should focus on these larger patterns, not on isolated or individual words and certainly not on nonsense words. Lefevre claims that the patterns of the written language reflect the patterns of the spoken language and that children must be taught to re-create the sounds of the original spoken patterns from the marks on the printed page. In order to do this they not only must be taught phoneme-grapheme correspondences but they also must be taught how to relate groups of written words to groups of spoken words and how to relate punctuation symbols to intonation patterns. Lefevre stresses the importance of teaching the child to re-create the stress and intonation of the spoken sentence that underlies the written sentence on the page before him. The re-created sentence must "sound right" to the child if he is to comprehend it. *Linguistics and the Teaching of Reading* is for the most part a presentation of the kind of linguistic knowledge that a teacher requires to be successful in helping a child to perform such a re-creation, but it has very little to say about how that task is to be performed by the child.

The insistence on the importance of the sentence unit in beginning reading is one of the new contributions that Lefevre makes to discussions of the possible uses of linguistic knowledge in the teaching of reading. Yet another important contribution is his insistence that an adequate approach to a theory of reading instruction must be interdisciplinary: linguists alone do not have all the answers, any more than do psychologists and educators. Linguists have too often made assertions about reading rather than offering hypotheses about it and have left important assumptions both unstated and unexamined. Almost every other point in what Lefevre calls his basic theory is either explicit or implicit in the book by Fries: the secondary character of writing; the control of language exhibited by five- to seven-year-olds; the need for teachers to avoid confusing statements about letters with statements about sounds; the avoidance of teaching about the language in favor of teaching language skills; and the need to consider skills in sequence. Lefevre's book is basically an elementary book on linguistics rather than a book on linguistics and reading and then only on a particular kind of linguistics, the structural linguistics of the 1950's. It is a successful book as far as it goes, because it offers teachers and researchers who are interested in language some basic understanding of a particular kind of linguistics. Linguistics has changed much in recent years, however, and the particular theory of linguistics put forward by Lefevre has given way to newer ones that probably have much more potential for reading teachers and reading researchers. The newer theories also recognize the importance of the sentence as the unit of language but treat it in a very different manner from Lefevre and within a very different framework from that used in *Linguistics and the Teaching of Reading*.

From the foregoing comments on the writings of Bloomfield, Fries, Soffietti, Hall, and Lefevre, it is obvious that many linguists have taken an interest in recent years in the teaching of reading and have tried to offer advice to reading experts and teachers on that subject. Devine (1966) points out that opinion has generally predominated over fact in the ensuing discussion of the various proposals. Nor does Devine find either side in the discussion to be without fault. Some of the reading experts such as Betts (1966) have voiced concern about the way linguists have dabbled in reading without investigating the complexity of the problems that arise in teaching reading. On the other hand it must be pointed out that reading experts have often dabbled in linguistics. Betts' article reveals his own preoccupation with the very concern that Lefevre is so critical of, the concern with word perception as the basis of reading. It seems inevitable, therefore, that linguists and reading experts have been unable to agree on the contribution linguistics can make to reading. Further problems result from the fact that linguists have different views about the nature of linguistic inquiry. Even when they agree as to what linguistic inquiry is properly all about, they interpret the relevance of their discoveries for reading instruction quite differently. Faced with such apparent confusion, therefore, reading teachers and researchers sometimes refuse to become involved with linguistics because there appears to be no large body of generally accepted information that is readily available to them. In actual fact there is considerable agreement among linguists about how languages can be studied. Linguistics is a lively discipline; consequently, its areas of controversy are much more apparent to the outsider than its areas of agreement.

It is probably true to say that linguists have not found the acceptance for their work or for derivative materials that they might have expected from the educated public. Reading teachers and researchers are part of that educated public, and they have reacted little differently from others to linguistic work. They too have tended to misunderstand and to be suspicious. There is also no reason to suppose that it is very easy for a reading teacher or reading researcher to unlearn what he has learned about language. A teacher or researcher who accepts linguistic findings would have to reject a considerable part of the tradition within which his co-workers function. He would accept the primacy of speech, realize that writing is a codification of speech, be descriptive rather than prescriptive, refuse to count and compute linguistically indefensible data, and insist on linguistically defensible bases for research. The result might well be that he would be rather isolated if he wanted to work in reading. It would be true to say that most reading experts have given only token recognition to linguistics in their work, with the consequence that the vast part of what is discussed under the name of linguistics in texts, methods, and courses on reading is in reality very far from the best linguistic knowledge that is available today. And it is just about as far from the kind of linguistic knowledge that has been available for many years now and that has been discussed in this chapter with particular reference to Bloomfield, Fries, and Lefevre.

CHAPTER THREE

The Nature of Linguistic Inquiry

The particular variety of linguistics we have been discussing for possible application to the teaching of reading is the one that dominated American linguistics from the early 1930's to the late 1950's. This variety is sometimes referred to as Bloomfieldian, descriptive, or structural. A descriptive or structural linguist usually defines a language as an arbitrary system of vocal symbols used for communication and considers his task to be one of describing that language by using certain procedures which allow him either to discover or to postulate its linguistic structure. He also attempts to characterize any such structure by employing such concepts as the phoneme, morpheme, immediate constituents, sentence patterns, and so on. These concepts are part of an arsenal of linguistic universals that he believes he can usefully employ in the study of any language, because they should enable the linguist to deal systematically and successfully with any problem that might arise in describing either the phonology or the grammar.

Using such an approach in writing a grammar of English, a linguist would be tempted to make statements such as the following:

1. English is a natural language and therefore shares certain

characteristics with all other natural languages, such as certain kinds of patterns and contrastive systems.

2. The language somehow exists in the utterances of speakers of English and cannot be described apart from these utterances.

3. In order to describe English it is necessary to observe the utterances of English speakers.

4. These utterances must be recorded accurately in a defensible system of recording—a phonetic system—and then the recorded data must be examined so that statements can be made about the structures in the data.

5. Certain analytical procedures applied to the data will allow the linguist to discover or to postulate the significant sounds (the phonemes), the significant meaning-bearing units (the morphemes), their combinations (the words), and the grammatical structures (the syntax).

6. The linguist's task is to write a phonology and a grammar of English that accurately describe the observed data and that at the same time recognize every contrastive feature and ignore every noncontrastive or redundant feature.

7. The linguist must be objective at all times, must keep opinions out of his work, both his informants' opinions and his own opinions, must use rigorous scientific procedures, and must strictly avoid any mentalistic diversions.

Essentially this approach, which has been called taxonomic, is one of collecting and classifying data according to certain principles that evolved over several decades. For a long while the merits of the approach outweighed by far its disadvantages. It was possible, for example, to describe English in a different way from those descriptions that had been organized within a framework originally developed to describe Latin. This Latinate framework, the typical model used for school grammars until very recently, forces English into a Latin mold, so that the student who says, "I never really understood my English grammar until I learned Latin" is in effect making a damning comment on what he has been taught about English and not a comment about Latin at all. Better descriptions of English than these Latinate ones were written during the period when Latinate grammars were widely used in schools, but these scholarly descriptions remained largely unknown to school teachers. The new structural descriptions provided them with the breakthrough that was needed.

The structural approach also made possible the use of the phonemic principle, that there is only a limited number of contrasting sounds or phonemes in any language, to gain an understanding of the sound patterns of English. There was never complete agreement, however, about how the principle was to operate or even about the reality of the phonemes that were to be discovered or postulated by employing the principle. Despite these problems, the concern with phonology did result in a renewed interest in spoken English, which in turn led to the discovery of the systematic differences among the many different dialects of English and to a study of the systematic relationships between the spoken and the written language, particularly between English pronunciation and orthography. Linguists also examined the traditional definitions of such terms as syllable, word, and sentence, particularly as these applied to the spoken language. This examination revealed both inadequacies in those definitions and certain difficulties in devising more suitable definitions. In morphology and syntax the previous preoccupation with meaning gave way to a concern for grammatical marking and distribution, for items and structures bearing different types of meaning, and for syntactic patterns. *Cat* is a noun because it can be pluralized as *cats* and not because it is a "name." *Old* is an adjective because it can be used in both slots in the sentence *The ―― man was very ――*. *The cat chased the rat* is a very different sentence pattern from either *Did the cat chase the rat?* (because it elicits a different type of response from the person to whom the remark is addressed) or *The cat died* (because the utterances have different constituent parts, subject–verb–object versus subject–verb). A structure such as *old wall* is a structure of modification like *stone wall* but the former employs the adjective *old* as the modifier of the noun *wall* whereas the latter employs the noun *stone* as the modifier of *wall*. Such illustrations could be expanded and made much more detailed, but these serve to indicate the differences between the Latinate approach and the newer structural or descriptive one. They also show some essential characteristics of the latter approach.

The structural approach stemming from Bloomfield should have provided a healthy antidote to the prevailing concern with the written language, to prescriptivism in teaching grammar, and to the dominant grammatical mythology. That the approach turned out to be unpalatable to many people, educators and educated public alike, was mainly the result of certain sociological factors, principally the kind of instruction about their language which the educated public had received. To some extent, however, the lack of acceptance resulted from the stance taken by some of the would-be popularizers of linguistics, whose excesses succeeded only in alienating people, not in winning them over. Faced with some of the overstatements of linguistic popularizers and unwilling to subject their received opinions to serious reexamination, many English professors, literary critics, editors, and influential writers resorted to ill-informed attacks on the new "scientism of language." In doing so, they either misinterpreted, misrepresented, or rejected the new approach to language study. Perhaps nothing less should have been expected because Bloomfield's linguistics was every bit as revolutionary in the 1930's as Chomsky's was to become in its turn a generation later. It is obviously not the fate of revolutionaries to be made to feel welcome by the establishment, whether that establishment is political, economic, social, or academic in nature.

Recent years have seen a reversion to some of the concerns that antedated Bloomfieldian linguistics as a result of the revolutionary proposals for linguistic study put forward by Chomsky in *Syntactic Structures* (1957). More recent works by Chomsky, mainly *Aspects of the Theory of Syntax* (1965) and *Cartesian Linguistics* (1966), have resulted in some changes of detail in the proposals he made in 1957 concerning the proper goals of linguistic inquiry, but the basic goals themselves have not changed. Moreover, they are widely recognized today as the goals that linguists should be pursuing. Prompted by Chomsky's theorizings, more and more linguists have begun to ask the same kinds of questions about language and linguistic theory that certain pre-Bloomfieldian universal grammarians asked. There is, however, at least one fundamental difference between these linguists and their predecessors: linguists today insist on far more explicit answers than did their predecessors, who had to accept less satisfactory answers because they did not have available the technical apparatus to make fully explicit, or formal, statements. This technical apparatus has only recently become available as a result of the developments in twentieth-century science and philosophy. The Bloomfieldians also tried to be explicit and rigorous in their procedures; that they failed to be so in many cases cannot be doubted, but such failures were almost certainly the result of asking questions which today many linguists would regard as unanswerable—questions such as, what *are* the phonemes of English if by phoneme one means such and such, or if phonemes may be discovered by following a certain procedure—rather than the result of deliberately sacrificing rigor. If rigor was occasionally sacrificed in favor of "pseudo-procedures," it was always to save time in making descriptions and never because of a lack of respect for rigorous procedures and statements. The questions that are now being asked in linguistics resemble many of those questions that have always been asked. It is likely that linguists now can provide better answers to these questions than any of their predecessors could, because recent advances in theory construction indicate both what kinds of questions are answerable and what forms acceptable answers should take.

Linguists are currently engaged in asking questions of the following kinds: What kind of linguistic system must speakers share so that they can produce and understand an infinite number of well-formed sentences? A tentative answer is that it must be a finite system of a particular kind that allows for the production of an infinite set of possibilities, because infinite systems could not be learned by finite speakers. However, what might such a finite system be like? How is it possible to account for the fact that listeners can detect ambiguities, nonsense sentences, and deviant sentences without any great difficulty? How can they also detect "foreign" accents, different dialects, slips of the tongue, possible words versus impossible words, new coinages, and so on? One answer to these questions might be that speaker-listeners have acquired some feeling for a "normal" use of their language. How can speakers distinguish between structured groups of sentences and sets of random sentences? Again the answer might be that there are patterns, either syntactic or semantic, which have domain over larger units than sentences and of which users of the language are aware. How is language acquired and why is it apparently acquired everywhere in very much the same way? Why do different languages apparently share many of the same features: sounds, morphemes, patterns?

There apparently must be certain linguistic universals, but what are they and why do they exist?

These questions are all very different from the questions asked by Bloomfieldian linguists, who would have rejected almost every one of them as either mentalistic or unanswerable and therefore quite outside the scope of linguistic inquiry as they conceived it. On the other hand, the pre-Bloomfieldian universal grammarians were quite prepared to give answers to most of these questions but their answers were inadequate. Linguists today insist that answers take a certain form. It is possible to answer most questions in many ways; in order to judge a particular answer it is therefore necessary to have some notion of what constitutes a better or a worse answer. Given two answers to a question, a linguist may consider one to be more economical, so economy might be one criterion he could use; or one might be more natural or more general or intuitively more satisfying than the other. He might even want to employ all of these criteria in judging the appropriateness of a particular answer. The interesting fact is that these various criteria will usually provide non-contradictory answers, so that the demands of economy, naturalness, generality, and intuitive satisfaction will generally be met by the same answer to a particular question. Recent work in linguistics reaches far beyond an account of observed data to provide a description of some kind of abstract system "behind" the data and even a tentative explanation of why that abstract system must have the form it has. Such a result as this is in direct contrast with the results of the Bloomfieldian attempts to cover only observed data as thoroughly as possible, and it also goes far beyond the inexplicit coverage of the statements offered by the universal grammarians.

In order for linguists to achieve one of their basic goals in writing grammars, to separate statements about specific instances from those about the underlying system behind those instances, it seems necessary to distinguish between linguistic *performance* and linguistic *competence*—that is, between what a speaker or hearer actually says or hears, and what he knows, the knowledge he somehow draws on in making or understanding utterances. It is this latter knowledge that particularly interests many linguists today. Obviously, it is a knowledge that speakers find difficult to verbalize, but the fact that they have such difficulty is no argument that they do not possess the knowledge in question. Neisser (1967) has written:

How can it be supposed that a man "knows" or "has" a grammar if he can give no account of it; if indeed, no fully adequate description of English grammar has ever been published? . . . That people speak grammatically without being able to describe their grammar is no more surprising than that they see without being perceptual theorists, or think in the absence of a theory of thinking. (p. 249)

Generative-transformational linguists are interested in writing grammars that characterize what speakers "know" about their language rather than grammars that merely classify those utterances actually produced in speech.

Generative-transformational linguists believe that a grammar must be something more than an inventory of utterances or some derived catalog of these utterances. Neither an inventory nor a catalog would offer much more than a set of observations about certain utterances. Neither would have very much to say about the linguistic abilities of the speakers and listeners involved. Spoken language contains many kinds of what can be called performance characteristics: it is marked by hesitations, stops and starts, reductions, elisions, mazes, back-tracking, and so on. The Bloomfieldians readily recognized that such problems existed. Although these linguists claimed to base their grammars entirely on descriptions of data, most actually did not attempt to deal with completely unedited data. One notable exception was Fries, who based his study of English grammar, *The Structure of English* (1952), on fifty hours of unedited telephone conversations involving a total of more than three hundred speakers. Generally linguists elicited citation forms, asked for short utterances, sought repetitions of these utterances, and avoided long texts wherever possible in order not to have to do too much "cleaning-up" of what data they did collect. Today generative-transformational linguists are sometimes accused of making up their data by inventing their own sentences, examples, and counter-examples. Such a procedure seems to be no more reprehensible than a previous procedure that focused on "clean" rather than "dirty" data—that is, on data carefully elicited rather than randomly observed.

Many linguists now insist that their concerns should not be with such data, "clean" or "unclean," but with the underlying facts, the system that underlies the data. This underlying system *is* the grammar of the language, and observed utterances are merely manifestations of this grammar being used by speakers with greater or less success. As speakers and listeners, we recognize mazes, stops and starts, memory limitations, and so on, for what they are—something apart from the underlying grammatical system. Consequently, in writing a grammar, linguists must rigidly exclude the effects of such variables, even though they cannot ignore them; they must filter out the underlying facts from them. It may even be said that when someone listens to utterances or reads sentences, he perceives what he hears or reads in terms of such an idealized system and does not react only to the data which he observes and to the noise in the communication channel. Listening and reading are not, therefore, simple recognition and matching operations; rather they are complex operations in which the listener or reader must reconstruct an idealized sentence for each sentence that he observes if he is to understand that sentence. Many linguists today believe that they should be concerned with writing grammars which characterize this underlying system, which are neither grammars of speech production nor of speech recognition but are neutral—between the two, as it were. Such grammars are sometimes called grammars of competence in that they attempt to represent that grammatical knowledge of a language which all speakers of the language may be expected to possess, even though in different situations individual speakers and listeners will use that knowledge differently so that their actual performance will vary considerably.

A linguist who desires to create a competence model is confronted with a variety of problems. All he ever observes is linguistic performance, and from this he must infer what linguistic competence is. There is little overt behavior of any kind that he can say is a direct manifestation of competence. A possible exception is behavior of the kind sometimes called mentalistic, as, for example, when a speaker says that a certain sentence is ungrammatical or ambiguous or a paraphrase of another sentence. Such behavior can be explained only by postulating that the speaker is drawing on an underlying competence. It quite often happens that the statements the linguist would want to include in his grammar to account for such observations are exactly the same ones that he would need to account for many other sentences that did not prompt such observations.

A precise grammar, one that exactly characterizes the linguistic competence underlying the observed behavior of speakers and listeners, consists of a set of fully explicit rules which produce, or generate, sentences and their grammatical descriptions. Since the grammar must account for all the possible sentences of a language, the very first rule, therefore, will take a sentence as an axiomatic starting point and say that sentence S consists of, or may be rewritten as, some two or more units (A, B, . . .). Additional rules will in turn rewrite these units according to a small set of conventions required in writing such grammars for all languages, therefore forming an important set of formal linguistic universals. The rules may be of different kinds. They may allow for options, as when A is rewritten as C (D) so that A can become either C or CD but not D, or for alternatives, as when G may be rewritten as $\begin{Bmatrix} I \\ J \end{Bmatrix}$ so that G can become either I or J but not IJ. For example, if in the rule A → C (D), A is *verb*, C is *get*, and D is *out*, then A → C is *verb* → *get*, and A → CD is *verb* → *get out*, but A → D is *verb* → *out*, which is not permissible. If in G → $\begin{Bmatrix} I \\ J \end{Bmatrix}$, G is *tense*, I is *past*, and J is *present*, then G → I or J but not IJ. *Tense* → *past* or *tense* → *present* but not *tense* → *past* and *present*, because no English verb tense can be both *past* and *present* at the same time.

Because the rules are fully explicit, every sentence may be assigned a description in terms of the particular formula used in its derivation. If:

$$S \longrightarrow A\ B$$
$$A \longrightarrow C\ (D)$$
$$B \longrightarrow E\ F$$
$$C \longrightarrow (G)\ H$$
$$G \longrightarrow \begin{Bmatrix} I \\ J \end{Bmatrix}$$

then six different sentences can result from an initial S in this language:

1

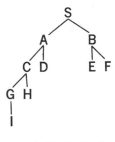

I H D E F

2

S
A   B
C D   E F
G H
J

J H D E F

3

S
A   B
C   E F
G H
I

I H E F

4

J H E F

5

H D E F

6

H E F

Various kinds of statements of a grammatical nature can be made about the resulting sentences. We may note that all have a basic A B structure; that in the first sentence A ultimately becomes I H D, whereas in the last A is ultimately rewritten to become just H alone; and that this particular grammar will produce the six sentences given above and no others.

A simple grammar for some English sentences might be as follows:

$$S \longrightarrow NP \ VP$$
$$NP \longrightarrow (D) \ N$$
$$VP \longrightarrow (Aux) \ Vb$$
$$Aux \longrightarrow \begin{Bmatrix} will \\ may \end{Bmatrix}$$
$$Vb \longrightarrow play$$
$$D \longrightarrow the$$
$$N \longrightarrow boys$$

This grammar accounts for the following six sentences only:

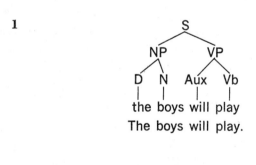

1

```
            S
          /   \
        NP      VP
       /  \    /  \
      D   N  Aux  Vb
      |   |   |    |
     the boys will play
```
The boys will play.

2

```
            S
          /   \
        NP      VP
       /  \    /  \
      D   N  Aux  Vb
      |   |   |    |
     the boys may play
```
The boys may play.

3

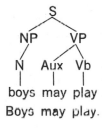

```
            S
         /     \
       NP       VP
       |       /  \
       N     Aux   Vb
       |      |    |
     boys    will  play
```

Boys will play.

4

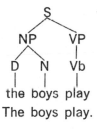

```
            S
         /     \
       NP       VP
       |       /  \
       N     Aux   Vb
       |      |    |
     boys    may  play
```

Boys may play.

5

```
            S
         /     \
       NP       VP
      /  \       |
     D    N     Vb
     |    |      |
    the  boys   play
```

The boys play.

6

```
            S
         /     \
       NP       VP
       |         |
       N        Vb
       |         |
     boys      play
```

Boys play.

The grammar allows us to say that both *boys* and *the boys* are NP's (noun phrases), that both *will* and *may* are Aux's (auxiliaries), that both *will play* and *may play* are VP's (verb phrases), and that *will may* is not a permissible sequence. A complete grammar of English would need many more rules than these few, but they would all be expressed in the same set of conventions.

By allowing the grammar to contain a rule of the following kind, which allows for the same symbol to appear to both the left and right of the arrow, in this case the symbol S:

$$S \longrightarrow A\ B\ (S)$$

we may build into the grammar the property of *recursiveness*, that is, the property of infinite expansion, as in the following sentence:

7

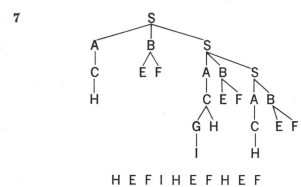

H E F I H E F H E F

In this example the initial S was rewritten as A B S and the S of this A B S was also rewritten as A B S. The final sentence H E F I H E F H E F is therefore derived from three different S's in an embedded structure which may alternatively be diagramed as follows:

vii

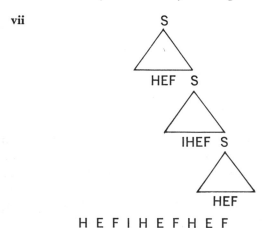

H E F I H E F H E F

An English sentence which has approximately the same embedded structures as the one just given is such a sentence as *I know John said he was sorry*, which can be diagramed as:

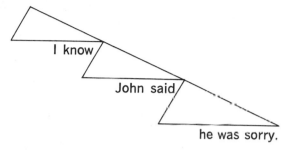

Some further examples from English will show how such rules operate. In the following set of sentences (8–10), the subject part of the sentence is filled by different groups of words which are an expanding set—*men, the men, some of the men:*

8   Men sing.
9   The men sing.
10 Some of the men sing.

In each case the sentence consists of two parts, a noun phrase and a verb phrase, actually a single verb in these examples. The verb phrase is always *sing* but the noun phrase is either a single noun (*men*), or a determiner and noun (*the men*), or a predeterminer, determiner, and noun (*some of the men*). In the next set of sentences (11–13), the important principle of recursiveness is illustrated in the modification of the adjective *old:*

11 He is old.
12 He is very old.
13 He is very, very old.

Quite obviously this set is capable of further expansion: *He is very, very, very, very . . . old.* Any limitation to the expansion derives from constraints in performance—that is, in finding a suitable occasion for the use of such an expansion—rather than in competence. No matter how may times *very* occurs between *He is* and *old,* the result must always be a grammatical sentence. The next set of sentences (14–16) includes a recursive set of modifiers of the noun *hat:*

14 John's hat disappeared.
15 John's wife's hat disappeared.
16 John's wife's cousin's hat disappeared.

In every case the noun phrase is fully grammatical; any limitation on the actual use of a particular noun phrase would be a performance limitation. It should be noted too that in each of these sets, 8–10, 11–13, and 14–16, it would be possible to continue the expansions even further, as in sentences 17–19:

17 Only some of the very old men sing.
18 He is very old, quite tired, rather bored, and obviously unhappy.
19 John's pretty wife's old male cousin's brown hat disappeared.

If this were all that current generative-transformational linguistic theory had to offer, it would be only a small improvement over older theories, because it would provide no more than a new procedure for writing very explicit phrase structure grammars—that is, grammars that attempt to assign the correct surface structures to sentences. But the theory does have considerably more to offer. In 1957 Chomsky effectively demonstrated in *Syntactic Structures* that even generative phrase structure grammars cannot adequately characterize natural languages. He claimed that it is necessary to postulate still more powerful grammars. Such grammars would require not only the use of rules and generative processes but also the use of transformational processes which would transform abstract deep phrase structures into the surface structures of actually observed sentences.

According to the new theory, every grammatical sentence has a deep phrase structure generated according to the phrase structure rules in the base of the grammar. This deep phrase structure is filled out with lexical items, or words, and then the various transformations of the language do or do not apply depending on the particular deep phrase structure in question. In current formulations of the theory all such transformations are obligatory. They serve to map out deep or underlying phrase structures—*deep* and *underlying* are interchangeable terms—into surface structures which can actually be pronounced or written. This principle of transformation from a deep structure to a surface structure may be illustrated by reference to the following sentences 20–22:

20 He was wounded.
21 I am going.
22 Who came?

The surface structures of these sentences are derived through transformations from abstract deep phrase structures (here greatly simplified for presentation) such as:

   xx   SOMENOUN   past   wound   he   PASSIVE
   xxi   I   present   progressive   go
   xxii   QUESTION   SOMEONE   past   come

In each case a transformation does or does not apply as an automatic consequence of the deep structure. In xx it is the presence of *PASSIVE* in the deep structure that results in the passive verb of 20. The deep subject *SOMENOUN* must be deleted, with the result that we understand that the *he* of 20 was wounded by "something" or "someone." The *SOMENOUN* element can underlie either of these indefinite pronouns. In xxi it is the presence of *progressive* in the deep structure that results in the production of *am going* in 21. In xxii it is the presence of *QUESTION* and *SOMEONE* in the deep structure that results in *Who* in 22. Transformations are quite automatic. A transformation must apply if the deep phrase structure is one to which it can apply. A transformation does not apply (is blocked) if the deep phrase structure is not exactly the one specified by the transformational rules. For example, the imperative transformation would not apply (would be blocked) in xx, xxi, and xxii, because the deep phrase structures contain neither the *IMPERATIVE* nor the *you present will* elements, both of which must be present in the deep structure for the imperative transformation to operate.

Transformations do not change one sentence into another sentence; they do not make active sentences into passive sentences or statements into questions, for example. Transformations change deep structures into surface structures, and every deep structure must undergo at least one transformation before it becomes a surface structure. Transformations add, delete, or rearrange elements in converting deep structures into surface structures. An addition occurs in such a case as the conversion of the deep structure xxiii into the surface structure 23; in this case the correct form of the element *be* is added:

xxiii   the   car   present   old
23   The car is old.

A deletion occurs in such a case as the conversion of the deep structure **xxiv** into the surface structure **24**; in this case *IMPERA-TIVE you present will* is deleted:

xxiv   IMPERATIVE   you   present   will   stand   up
24   Stand up!

A rearrangement occurs in such a case as the conversion of the deep structure **xxv** into the surface structure **25**; in this case the *past   be* is preposed to the subject noun phrase and *QUESTION* is deleted:

xxv   QUESTION   John   past   be   a   success
25   Was John a success?

It must be noted in every case that the addition, deletion, or rearrangement does not affect the meaning of the sentence. *Meaning is almost entirely a property of the deep structures of sentences and of the lexical items in the deep structures.* If one understands *Who?* in sentence **22**, it is because he "knows" that *Who?* is derived from a deep structure containing *QUESTION SOMEONE.* It is exactly this kind of knowledge that a generative-transformational grammar attempts to characterize.

As we have seen, transformations change deep structures into surface structures. The lexical items in a sentence—that is, the words—are introduced into the deep structure before transformations turn the whole of the deep structure and the lexical content into a surface structure. As the final part of the whole process, a set of phonological rules comes into operation to provide the surface structure with a *phonetic representation,* so that, for example, *cat   plural* becomes [kæts], *dog   plural* becomes [dɔgz], and *mouse   plural* becomes [maɪs]. Because the rules that convert deep structures into phonetic representations bring in everything that is predictable in the language, and because it is possible to write a great many of these rules, the deep structures need contain only those features that are absolutely necessary to trigger the transformational rules. For example, *long* as a free form and *long* as part of *longer* are pronounced differently: [lɔŋ] and [lɔŋg]. The deep structure can show the underlying form to be the same //long//, however, because the surface difference can be accounted for by transformational rules that make the nasal consonant //n// homorganic (made in the same position) to the stop consonant //g// and then delete the //g// before a word boundary. Similarly, in the deep structure it is unnecessary to specify the first consonant in *spread* as anything but a consonant, or the penultimate consonant in *lamp* as anything but a nasal, or the first vowels in *nation* and *national* as anything but a single vowel //a//, because low level phonological rules apply automatically to produce the different phonetic results.

It is possible to make certain observations about this kind of grammatical model:

1. Every surface sentence may be assigned at least one grammatical description. If it may be assigned more than one, it is a grammatically ambiguous sentence; that is, it may be derived from more than one deep structure. Sentences 26 and 27 are ambiguous sentences:

26 The shooting of the hunters disturbed us.
27 Time flies

Sentence 26 is ambiguous because it may be derived from either of two deep structures, xxvia or xxvib:

xxvia IT (the hunters past shoot SOMETHING) past disturb we
xxib IT (SOMENOUN past shoot the hunters) past disturb we

Likewise, sentence 27 can be derived from either xxviia or xxviib:

xxviia time present fly
xxviib IMPERATIVE you present will time flies

2. Every surface sentence is interpretable only by reference to its deep structure. In order to comprehend a sentence, one must provide that sentence with a reading for its deep structure and lexical content. This reading of syntax and semantics provides the meaning of the sentence; the surface sentence has a surface structure and is a phonetic representation of this deep content, but these provide no more than the raw data for processing. This act of processing is the act of comprehension.

3. Every surface sentence is a realization in phonological (or graphological) substance of a basic reality, an underlying structure. These surface features, such as the voicing contrast in the final sibilants of [kæts] and [dɔgz], the stress contrast in *élement* and *eleméntary*, and the vowel reduction in *man* [mæn] and *postman* [mən], are always predictable from the deep structure.

4. It is possible to assign a deep structure to every grammatical sentence, no matter how long. It is possible to account for every grammatical sentence in terms of the model and to explain intuited relationships among sentences by reference to the model. For example, a sentence like *The young boy is helping the injured man* can be shown to be a complex sentence containing three sentences: *The boy is helping the man, The boy is young,* and *SOMENOUN injured the man.* Likewise, an ungrammatical sentence is ungrammatical because it cannot be assigned a deep structure.

It is important to reemphasize one crucial point about grammar and rules. The grammar and its rules are not a characterization of performance. They are not intended to be a model of how sentences are actually produced or understood by speakers—that is, a model of what speakers actually do in constructing sentences. The rules are not rules of behavior, nor do they have any necessary psychological correlates. Grammars *generate* sentences and descriptions; speakers *produce* sentences; *generate* and *produce* are not synonymous. It may eventually prove to be the case that the rules do correlate closely with psychological processes, but at the present time no such correlation is claimed for them. It may be the case, too, that a competence model of language underlies a performance model of language in some very simple way, but so far it is not at all clear how linguistic competence relates to the various kinds of linguistic performance. Much of a recent conference (Lyons and Wales, 1966) was devoted to this particular problem, the relationship of competence to performance, but the participants were unable to agree exactly on the precise relationship between the two. The problem is an extremely complex one. Given the present state of knowledge about both linguistics and psychology, it would be well to treat with considerable skepticism any claim that a generative-transformational model of the kind presently in use actually does form a substantial part of a model of linguistic performance.

Linguists are currently engaged in a type of linguistic inquiry far different from that of a decade ago. Even linguists who are not generative-transformationalists are engaged in very much the same types of inquiry, though their starting points and their approaches to the problems are quite different. There is nearly everywhere in linguistics a great interest in formal systems and in the universal properties of languages. Likewise, there is an interest in specifying exactly what a linguistic description must include and what its "power" should be, what demands it must meet. Finally, there is an obvious concern with meaning and semantics, in particular with accounting for how sentences achieve the meanings they do achieve. This type of inquiry is far different from that which has been characterized as linguistic so far in the discussions of possible applications of linguistics to reading. The time is obviously ripe, then, to examine reading from the perspective of current linguistic knowledge.

CHAPTER FOUR

Some Linguistic Insights into Reading Instruction

When a person reads, he is processing information. Information processing itself is an activity common to all living organisms. Every living organism must learn to deal with its environment if it is to survive, and it must learn to react to a variety of external stimuli. It is useful to characterize this reaction process in the terms of information processing: signals, noise, channel, code, message, and so on. The organism must learn to distinguish important variables from unimportant ones in its environment—that is, distinguish signals from noise—and must be able to interpret these variables in some way, to react to them as messages in some code or other proceeding over a channel to which the organism is attuned. When a human being reads, he is carrying out a kind of information processing that no other organism can perform. Yet the general processing activities involved are not very different from those employed by other organisms or by the same human being in other tasks. Rather, a unique and complicated integration of information processing abilities is required. It is desirable, therefore, to discover the extent to which reading is a special type of information processing in order to point out some of its unique characteristics and, consequently, its unique potential problems.

By the time a child is confronted with the task of learning to read, he has already learned to use his different senses in order to come to terms with his environment. For example, he has already learned to do such things as judging distances and differentiating among objects. He has already learned to react only to the significant contrastive features, or the criterial attributes, of objects in his environment and to ignore non-contrastive features. Both Cadillacs and Volkswagens are "cars," even though they might appear to have more differences than similarities; the differences are noise and the similarities are signals to the child, so that both are "cars." Likewise "Mom" is still "Mom" for a child, even though she is wearing slacks, pictured in a photograph, or costumed for a masquerade. In learning to read, however, a child must master a completely new set of visual tasks and must learn to relate this learning to certain oral-aural learning that has already taken place. He must also go beyond this level of success, because as he develops skill in reading, he will be called upon to develop very subtle and quite new types of information processing which are unique to reading: such advanced reading skills as skimming, inferential reading, critical reading, proofreading, and so on.

The term *information processing* is deliberately chosen, and such terms as information theory and communication theory are deliberately avoided. Information and communication theory, as discussed by such writers as Shannon and Weaver (1949), are theories which have a certain utility for characterizing a communication system; they are, however, basically mathematical models designed to account for the location of information in messages. Messages are considered to be describable as chains of items of varying predictability, such that the amount of information supplied by any item varies directly with its unpredictability from context. Therefore, in a particular environment, an easily predicted item conveys less information than an item less easily predicted. For example, when any one of a set of six possibilities can occur in a particular environment, then the occurrence of one of the six possibilities provides more information than would be the case if the environment allowed for only two possibilities, not six. If after *ac* any one of *x, p, o, s, l,* and *b* can occur, then *a c o* conveys much more information than it would in a case where only *p* or *o* can occur after *ac*. In the first case, six different possibilities exist, whereas in the latter there are but two possibilities. It is for this reason—that it is much less predictable—that the first *o* conveys more information than the second *o*.

Such a model does have some limited uses in helping one to understand how the information conveyed in sentences is either conveyed or processed. It is well known that certain sounds, letters, words, and even whole sentences can not infrequently be predicted from context. For example, the completions of *thoug–*, *Open your books and begin* ——, and *How do you do?* ——, are highly predictable. They are very likely to be *h, reading,* and *Very well, thank you,* respectively. It is instructive to compare this high predictability with the low predictability of the completions of: *ca–*, *He went to the* ——, and *Why did you do it?* ——. Chomsky (1957), however, rather conclusively demonstrated that even though such a model has many uses, it nevertheless proves to be an inadequate characterization for a natural language. Sentences are not just simple left-to-right sequences of elements. It is impossible to offer adequate characterizations of the structures of sentences with a model that employs transitional probabilities alone. It might be possible to develop a model to account for, or generate, all possible English sentences, actually an infinite set, but the model would also generate another infinite set of ungrammatical sentences. The dependencies among words in sentences in natural languages are subtle and sometimes distant, as, for example, between *books* and *are* in *The* books *that you left over at John's house before you went on your vacation last summer* are *still there.* A model based on transitional probabilities capable of allowing this sentence to be produced would be fantastically complicated (if indeed it were possible); it would also produce more ungrammatical sequences than grammatical ones. Since a grammar should generate only grammatical sentences, the inadequacy of such a model as a grammar is clear.

Just as it is not possible to account for how sentences are structured on a simple linearity principle, so it proves inadequate to use such a principle to explain how sentences are understood. Sentences are not understood as a result of adding the meaning of the second word to that of the first, the third to the first two, and so on. The statement by Spache (1964, p. 12) that "in its simplest form, reading may be considered a series of word perceptions" is quite inadequate. There are many other dependencies that are important in understanding sentences, and these are not arranged in a simple linear or serial fashion. Sentences have a "depth" to them, a depth which grammatical models such as phrase structure models and generative-transformational models attempt to represent. These models suggest that if a left-to-rightness principle is relevant to sentence processing, it must be a left-to-rightness of an extremely sophisticated kind that requires processing to take place concurrently at several levels, many of which are highly abstract: phonological or graphological, structural, and semantic. Consequently, many different types of perception and many different types of dependency are involved. The reader, for example, must concurrently perceive letter shapes and the relationship of these to surrounding letter shapes, combine letter shapes into words, combine words into grammatical structures, and deal with semantic collocations which "make sense" in the general context of the passage being read. In effect, to consider such complex processing in terms of left-to-rightness seems particularly unrevealing.

In discussing the possible application of information theory to the study of language function, Neisser (1967) writes:

> . . . I do not believe, however, that this approach was or is a fruitful one. Attempts to quantify psychological processes in informational terms have usually led, after much effort, to the conclusion that the "bit rate" is not a relevant variable after all. Such promising topics as reaction time, memory span, and language have all failed to sustain early estimates of the usefulness of information measurement. (p. 7)

He points out that the "bit," the unit of measurement used by information theorists, was developed to study unselective systems. Human beings, however, are selective. They are active, not passive. Reading is but one of the active types of processing in which they indulge.

The information processing model, as distinct from the information theoretic model, is useful in discussing language and reading. For example, it is obvious that the information processing involved in reading may break down in several places, particularly in the beginning stages of reading, where there are many new processing techniques to be learned and new relationships to be established. Beginning readers may lack the ability to recognize letter shapes and to discriminate between them. Inexperienced readers may not have acquired, or may not easily acquire, knowledge of permissible letter combinations. In later stages students may misread letter and word sequences as a result of ignorance—that is, as a result of the complete novelty of the material—or as a result of trying to use inappropriate structural, semantic, or contextual information. They may also have difficulties with lexical items: omitting, transposing, supplying them; they may not be able to handle certain grammatical structures with ease, they may misinterpret particular semantic collocations, and they may utilize contexts incorrectly.

One task the learner faces in beginning to read is that of linking contrasting visual symbols to the significant acoustic contrasts with which he is already familiar, which he already, therefore, "knows." At the same time, however, he must also learn to react only to the significant characteristics of these symbols. Like the allophonic variants of phonemes, these symbols vary in different contexts: capital versus lower case, different type faces, printing versus writing, and so on, so the beginning reader must learn to disregard the noise associated with such differences and react to the significant "g" characteristics of a *g* (G G g g *g*) and the significant "a" characteristics of an *a* (A A *a* a a), rather than to the non-significant variations of particular styles and conventions of printing or writing.

There is considerable literature on the perception of shapes, based on many psychological experiments, which discusses the problem in terms of "recognition," "matching," "categorization," "stimulus generalization," and "critical attributes," to cite but a few of the terms developed by psychologists.

The child learning to read must also acquire a new set of expectations regarding frequencies. These will be mainly graphological frequencies having to do with combinations such as *wh, qu, gh, th, ei, ow, igh,* and so on, but to a lesser extent they will be also semantic and syntactic frequencies, as the written language diverges in content and structure from the spoken language. These syntactic and semantic differences will demand that the reader learn to process different messages from those he has processed in speech. By its very nature much of the content of writing is different from that of speech, because writing allows for (and on occasion demands) a more deliberate kind of language than does speech. The utterances of the spoken language are generally far less edited than the sentences of the written language, as the following examples show. The first two are from Strickland (1962); they illustrate the "run-on" nature characteristic of the language of many children:

1. I used to have another dog and its name was Peanut but it got run over by a car and now I have another one and its name is Crickett and I have a big dog and its name is Shauntesy and the little dog always follows around Shauntesy. (p. 26)

2. Then after we went to Santa Claus Land we took a drive to Lincoln State Park on the way back and when we went we went to this log hut and we got to see the first house that Abraham Lincoln lived in and the only thing left was the fireplace cause it fell down but they cleared out all the junk and the chimney was the only thing that was left. (p. 26)

The third is from a conversation between adults recorded by Dixon (1965), slightly rearranged for presentation here:

3. A. I'm—I, I have a proposition to make to you—er well to all of you—or whoever's here at Christmas.
   J. What?
   A. And that is that I'll provide a bird—if you can cook it.
   J. Where?—Here?
   A. Anywhere.
   J. Oh well I'll cook here—I, I'm . . .
   A. Well no my mother said she'd send me a bird—and I don't know whether she said a cooked bird—or an uncooked bird.
   J. I'm not coming up to your poke to cook it—where I have to stick with my hair out of the window—before I can sort of get near the oven—I'll cook it here for you.
   A. Oh you will—I mean but you've got to do everything else to it I mean.
   J. All the trimmings I know.
   A. A—a—and the potatoes and all the rest.
   J. Yeah of course. (p. 202)

The fourth is part of a telephone conversation from Fries (1952):

4. I wanted to tell you one more thing I've been talking with Mr. D—— in the purchasing department about our typewriter (yes)

that order went in March seventh however it seems that we are about eighth on the list (I see) we were up about three but it seems that for that type of typewriter we're about eighth that's for a fourteen-inch carriage with pica type (I see) now he told me that R——'s have in stock the fourteen-inch carriage typewriters with elite type (oh) and elite type varies sometimes it's quite small and sometimes it's almost as large as pica (yes I know) he suggested that we go down and get Mrs. R—— and tell her who we are and that he sent us and try the fourteen-inch typewriters and see if our stencils would work with such type (I see) and if we can use them to get them right away because they have those in stock and we won't have to wait (that's right) we're short one typewriter right now as far as having adequate facilities for the staff is concerned (yes) we're short and we want to get rid of those rentals (that's right) but they are expecting within two weeks or so to be receiving—ah—to start receiving their orders on eleven-inch machines with pica type (oh) and of course pica type has always been best for our stencils (yes) but I rather think there might be a chance that we can work with elite type (well you go over and try them and see what they're like and do that as soon as you can so that we'll not miss our chance at these). (pp. 50–51)

The above examples should confirm the fact that almost any kind of writing other than the transcription of unrehearsed spoken utterances involves a certain amount of "editing": one has only to look closely at verbatim records of child or adult language, of discussions, and of unrehearsed dialogs to realize how heavily edited is the kind of written material we usually read. Writing is not just speech written down!

The beginning reader is called upon to develop additional intuitions about this new language experience, and even though many of his old intuitions continue to be relevant, they are not by themselves adequate for this task. It must, however, be emphasized that his new intuitions have to be related to a sensory system, his visual one. The child must acquire new neuromuscular coordination, such as eye movements of a particular kind, and, if one holds to theories of "silent speech," he must coordinate such movements with either overt or covert articulating movements. He must also become aware of completely new varieties of linguistic performance, the varieties of written language that are not the same as those of speech. In such circumstances it is to be expected that some children will experience difficulties in learning to read and that these difficulties will be of different kinds and will require different kinds of solutions.

Just as in listening and speaking a person takes something to his task, so he must in reading: he takes a knowledge of English structure, not necessarily a knowledge that he can verbalize but an intuitive knowledge that he can draw upon. The accomplished reader takes an ability to process written symbols in a left-to-right fashion, a special kind of visual and motor ability; he also takes an awareness, though not necessarily again a conscious one, of the subtle differences between speech and writing: the stops, starts, mazes, and so on of the former in contrast with the controlled, edited sentences of the latter. Both the beginning reader and the accomplished reader also take to their reading a knowledge of the world. They have both lived and have come to some kind of terms with their environments, so that they can expect what they are reading to be generally meaningful and to be neither random data nor nonsensical nor ungrammatical. They may also expect that what they are required to read has meaning for them as individuals and that it is related to their needs and the kind of information they really want to process. Consequently, both the beginning reader and the sophisticated reader may expect to read largely within the area of meaning with which they are familiar and in which they are interested. It would appear to be an important function of the teaching of reading to lure readers into the relatively unknown, onto the byways as well as the highways, to enlarge the areas of meaning with which they are familiar. The proper rate of such a deliberate expansion of interest is again a pedagogical matter, not a linguistic one, but the linguist can contribute the information that the semantic components of most of the meanings that have to be acquired are already known intuitively by fairly young children. What the child finds necessary in new learning is to become aware of new combinations of these components.

If the preceding comments constitute a valid statement about the nature of the reading process, it would be appropriate to indicate what the linguist has to contribute to an understanding of the task of teaching children to read. What is there in linguistics that might help a teacher of reading to do that job better? What should the teacher know about language and the language processes involved in reading? What linguistic factors must be taken account of by researchers in their work on reading? Certain points emerge:

1. The linguist can offer some account of the linguistic competence presumably shared by mature users of the language. He can also point out how the actual observed linguistic performance of people varies from this competence. He might not, as a linguist, be able to say why it does vary, because the factors that cause it to vary are many and have to do mainly with various kinds of psychological constraints. However, the idea of linguistic competence itself—the idea that it is possible to characterize a linguistic system that every speaker of a language shares—is an extremely important contribution.

2. The linguist can offer characterizations of the linguistic competence of children at different stages of their language development. He can also characterize many aspects of the total language learning process. It is extremely important that children who are learning to read be given credit for what they already know intuitively about their language, even though they may not be able to verbalize this knowledge. By the age of six every normal child has learned to control a very complicated linguistic system, a system so complicated, in fact, that all the linguists who have attempted to write English grammars have still accounted for only *part* of it. Moreover, the six-year-old child has *learned* this system by himself; he has not been *taught* it. At various stages his control of the system has exhibited different kinds of phonological contrasts, syntactic patterns, and lexical selections from those of mature adult language. Nevertheless, at each stage it was a system, and not just a random set of responses nor an inadequate version of adult language. The linguist can offer help to teachers of reading in coming to an understanding of the language acquisition process. He can also point out that the normal child acquires language mainly as a result of his own efforts. Even though adults are in the habit of repeating utterances to children, exaggerating intonation contours, slowing down the rate of speech, simplifying sentence structures, overarticulating, and correcting "mistakes," such promptings to children are so random and the whole learning task so complicated that the most adequate hypothesis in the circumstances is that the child learns to talk, not

that he is taught to talk. The linguist, therefore, can point out the important differences between learning a language (it is doubtful if you can stop a normal child learning a language) and teaching a language (it is doubtful if this can be done at all) and between knowing a language (everybody who speaks English knows English intuitively or he could not speak it) and knowing about English (an academic matter, perhaps with only a tenuous connection to intuitive knowledge).

3. In his competence model the linguist can offer descriptions of the sentences of English, descriptions of the deep structure, semantic content, and phonology of each sentence. The linguist can thereby delineate for each sentence a major part of what must be involved in understanding that sentence—that is, what meanings and types of meaning are present in the sentence and, in the case of a written sentence, just how the symbols on paper relate to or realize these meanings. He is therefore able to relate the deep and surface structures of sentences to each other and show how understanding must take place at the level of the former rather than the latter. He is also able to show how surface structures may be realized in both speech and writing and may themselves be subject to various performance factors.

4. The linguist can offer an account of the systematic way in which symbols are used to represent linguistic structures. For example, writing is often said to be speech put down on paper. While it certainly proves fruitful to examine written English in this way, it is no less fruitful to examine written English itself as a kind of direct manifestation of a level of deep structure and to ignore any level of phonological representation. Certainly, if one wishes to understand the language processes involved in highly efficient "speed" reading, it may be unrealistic to postulate an intermediate stage of either overt or covert vocalization—that is, a stage of phonological representation.

5. The linguist can offer some help in explaining the semantic structures that exist in English. Recent years have seen a considerable increase in the interest taken by linguists in meaning, particularly in the subtle and, for linguists, challenging relationship of semantics and syntactics. This interest is partly the result of syntactic exploration, but it also arises from a realization that a complete study of a language requires a study of the semantic relationships

in that language. A concern with deep structure also demands such a study. The notion of deep structure is a valuable one, but it creates a problem in defining the term *deep*. How deep is deep? Various depths have been proposed, but in every case there is an apparent need to postulate different levels of linguistic organization from the level of observed sentences, particularly a level concerned with both syntax *and* semantics. It may not, therefore, be possible to answer the question about depth. The notion itself is no less valuable for that fact.

6. The linguist can offer descriptions of dialect variations; he can demonstrate the relationship of a particular spoken dialect to a standard written language; and he can provide some help in understanding the notion of "standard" language itself.

It is insights such as these which the linguist can offer to the reading teacher or reading researcher. It should be noted that these insights are linguistic in nature, not pedagogical. The linguist can point out that *pat* and *bat* are a minimal pair, just as are *bat* and *bet,* but he takes off his linguistic cap and puts on a pedagogical one when he says that in teaching reading *pat* should be taught in contrast with *bat* and that *bat* should be taught in contrast with *bet*. The linguist can say that in the writing system [ai] is generally represented as *y* before a space, as *igh* in certain morphemes, or as *i-* consonant *-e* in others, and he can even calculate the various frequencies of representation. However, when he says that the sound [ai] or the /ay/ contrast should be taught in association with one particular spelling before it is taught with others, he is no longer a linguist but a pedagogue. He is no longer describing but prescribing. He must realize that a pedagogical decision has to be made not on the basis of linguistic information alone but also on the basis of other kinds of information. The linguist may be qualified to contribute a linguistic *perspective* to the teaching of reading, but he cannot set out a linguistic *method* for teaching reading, because there can be no such method.

CHAPTER FIVE

Grammar and Reading

Grammarians have long been concerned with how sentences make sense, but until recently they were unable to be very explicit about the actual "sense-making" process. Lacking any notion of what constitutes a formal definition of a sentence—that is, one which is based on an explicit theory about how a language should be described—most grammarians were unable to separate grammatical statements from semantic ones and to avoid circular definitions. Today, it is quite apparent that definitions such as "a sentence is a group of words which makes sense," "a declarative sentence makes a statement," "a sentence expresses a complete thought," "a sentence begins with a capital letter and ends with a period" really say nothing at all because they avoid the real issue of specifying just what constraints a group of words must actually meet to make sense, to be declarative, to express a complete thought, and to be punctuated in a certain way. It is just such constraints that should be the concern of the grammarian.

Bloomfieldian linguists deliberately avoided such empty definitions and concentrated on describing what we have referred to as the surface structures of sentences. For example, they described such characteristics as intonation contours and syntactic patterns, showing the differences among such sentences as **1**, **2**, and **3** in terms of stress, pitch, and final pitch contour configurations:

1 He's HAPpy.
2 HE's happy.
3 He's HAPpy?

Sentence 1 has main stress on the adjective and a final falling pitch contour, so it stresses the point that the person spoken of is happy rather than in some other emotional state. Sentence **2**, with stress on the pronoun and a final falling pitch contour, stresses the identity of the person, not the emotion. Sentence **3**, with stress on the adjective and a final rising pitch contour, expresses some disbelief about the emotional state of the person spoken of. Bloomfieldians also described the differences among such sentences as **4–10** in terms of different sentence patterns:

4 The cat ate the mouse.
5 The cat slept.
6 The cat was content.
7 The cat is a pet.
8 The cat is here.
9 The man gave the cat some milk.
10 The cat has a collar.

Sentence **4** contains a transitive verb and one object, sentence **5** contains an intransitive verb and no object, sentences **6, 7,** and **8** contain *be* and different complements, sentence 9 contains a transitive verb and two objects, and sentence **10** contains a verb that appears to be transitive because of the apparent object but is not. (*A collar is had by the cat* is impossible. Linguists use an asterisk to mark such impossible or ungrammatical sentences.)

A Bloomfieldian linguist trying to produce an adequate definition of an English sentence would refer to such characteristics as these, or to structures such as predication, complementation, subordination, coordination, and modification. He would attempt to avoid references to any kind of meaning except differential meaning—that is, whether or not something is a repetition of a previous utterance. He would also assume that any corpus of utterances produced by a native speaker of English would be almost entirely grammatical. The linguist's task was to classify these utterances as sentence types and to describe their grammatical composition so that he could eventually investigate how meaning was conveyed in the language. An understanding of grammatical meaning as represented by intonation contours, sentence patterns, structures, or slot-filler correlations, however, was to be basic to any understanding of meaning in general. Most recently, linguists have gone beyond these concerns and have involved themselves with other aspects of the well-formedness of sentences, particularly with the subtle relationship of syntax to meaning itself, and also with grammatical structures of a more abstract kind than those that are overtly manifested in the surface representations of sentences.

If a person is to understand what is involved in the comprehension of any particular sentence, he must be conscious of its total linguistic content. On the other hand, to comprehend the sentence he is merely required to be a native speaker. The distinction again is between "knowing about" (understanding comprehension) and "knowing" (comprehending). Teachers of comprehension need to "know about" comprehension so they can understand what is involved in teaching it. The linguist can help them acquire this knowledge so necessary to their teaching.

Complete comprehension occurs when the recipient of a message becomes aware of the total content of that message. Total content in this sense means something like the exact message intended by the sender. Part of that content is, of course, hardly subject to a linguistic analysis. Take, for example, sentence 11:

11   John Smith was born in 1932.

The identity of *John Smith* is a non-linguistic identity. It is a referential identity, and unless the recipient of the message has some knowledge of who *John Smith* is, the full content of the message must escape him. An inspection of the sentence does, however, reveal that *John Smith* is marked grammatically as "animate," since only animates may be born. Such a fact is certainly true of any normal language use, because a sentence such as *The idea was born* is transparently metaphoric. It is also possible to say that some other "animate" bore John Smith, since the person in question is in a very important sense the object of an underlying sentence xi:

xi   SOME PERSON   past   bear   John   Smith   in   1932

In the actual surface structure of sentence 11, *John Smith* is the surface or grammatical subject; however, it is a deep object as indicated in xi. In the same way it is possible to compare sentences 12 and 13, in which the relationship between the subject and verb in the surface structures is quite different; the "agent" subject in 12 is also the deep subject, while the subject as "undergoer" in 13 is actually the deep object:

12   The woman washed the floor.
13   The floor was washed by the woman.

A sentence such as *John Smith was born in 1932* obviously has a great deal of grammatical content that must be understood if the sentence is to be comprehended. Comprehension requires far more than understanding the meanings of individual words and then fusing these meanings by some mysterious process so that sense will result. It is this process, this fusion itself, that requires a close examination. It has syntactic and semantic components, about which the linguist can provide important information.

A close examination of a small number of English sentences will show how important it is for anyone who wishes to understand the process of comprehension to be aware of the precise grammatical content of the sentences to be comprehended. Such an examination will also indicate that sentence comprehension requires much more than the recognition of a small number of surface sentence structures or various permutations of these structures, as structural grammarians tended to suggest it did. In addition to recognizing the superficial pattern or surface structure of a sentence, a listener or reader must project a deep structure for the sentence. Consequently, it is not enough for a linguist to list or to classify, no matter how exhaustively, the surface sentence structures in the hope that such a taxonomy will explain what needs to be explained about sentence interpretation. Such a taxonomy can do no more than record in a systematic way what a trained person can observe; it cannot explain how individual structures relate to each other or why different native speakers consistently have the same intuitions about certain linguistic matters. The surface structures of sentences undoubtedly are important; they certainly provide listeners and readers with the substance from which underlying forms are to be processed and they definitely have an important role to play in helping listeners and readers reconstruct the deep structures that underlie them. But it is at the level of deep structure that sentences actually must be interpreted, not at the level of surface structure.

The grammatical structure of sentence **14** should contain few obstacles to comprehension, because the deep structure **xiv** and the surface structure **14** are very like each other; the transformations that derive the second from the first have resulted in only one important change—a rearrangement:

14 The man took the book.

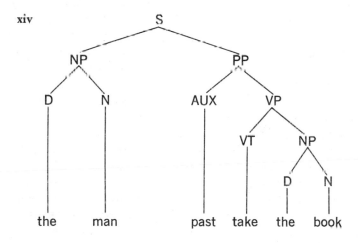

xiv

Even though the problem of understanding the deep structure of **14** is a relatively minor one, it must be pointed out that the comprehension of this simple sentence requires that *man* be interpreted as a noun (N) which together with a determiner *the* (D) constitutes a noun phrase (NP); that in this sentence this NP functions as the subject of the sentence (S) since it is the NP immediately under S; that in the phrase *took the book*, which is the sentence predicate (PP), *took*, a transitive verb (VT), is the past tense form of *take* because of the tense (T) and the auxiliary (AUX); and that *the book* is like *the man* in its structure, an NP, but in this case the noun phrase is the object of a verb within a verb phrase rather than the subject of a sentence. Additional observations could be made about sentence **14**, but these are the most relevant for present purposes.

Sentence 15 contains potentially more problems than 14 because its deep structure is very different from its surface structure:

15   The book was taken by the man.
xv   the   man   past   take   the   book   PASSIVE

In this example and the following ones, the tree-like structure used for the deep structure is omitted for purposes of further simplification; every grammatical sentence, however, must be regarded as having a tree-like deep structure of the same general form as indicated in xiv. In the deep structure of sentence 15, *the man* is the subject and *the book* is the object. These noun phrases must be understood to have such functions if a proper reading is to be given to the sentence. It is the presence of the *PASSIVE* element, or formative, in the deep structure that accounts for the transformational change, in this case an addition and a rearrangement, between the deep and surface structures. The result is that *the book* becomes the surface subject, *the man* becomes part of the phrase *by the man,* and the verbal element becomes *was taken.* The surface structure of the sentence provides clues to its interpretation; the interpretation itself depends on a correct processing of these clues to reconstruct all the elements and relationships of the deep structure. Sentences are perceived at the level of surface structure, but they are comprehended only at the level of deep structure.

Sentence 16 shows a considerable resemblance to sentence 15:

16   The book was taken.

There is an important difference between sentences 16 and 15, however. Sentence 16 provides no information about who or what took the book. Sentence 16 actually has a deep structure rather different from that of sentence 15; it may be represented as follows:

xvi   SOMENOUN   past   take   the   book   PASSIVE

SOMENOUN is a dummy element, an element that must be postulated as existing at the level of deep structure in a full account of the grammar of English. Such dummy elements are necessary to explain certain peculiarities of surface structure. The combination of *SOMENOUN* and *PASSIVE* results in the presence of the passive form of the verb and the deletion of the deep subject in the surface sentence as a result of obligatory transformational processes. These transformations apply whenever the structure is appropriate. The presence of the **PASSIVE** triggers a rearrangement transformation and an addition transformation, and the presence of **SOMENOUN** in a *by* phrase in the resulting string triggers a deletion transformation. These facts are sketched below:

> [Initial string: deep structure]
>
> xvi SOMENOUN past take the book PASSIVE
> [Passive transformation: rearrangement and addition of *be en*]
> the book past be en take by SOMENOUN
> [Deletion transformation]
> the book past be en take
> [Affix transformation: rearrangement]
> the book be past take en
> [Final sentence: surface structure]
>
> 16 The book was taken.

Each of the following sentences contains a negative element:

17 The man didn't take the book.
18 The book wasn't taken by the man.

These sentences show a considerable difference in the surface structures of their predicate phrases, with *did take* in 17 and *was taken* in 18; the deep structures, however, show a basic similarity:

> xvii NOT the man past take the book
> xviii NOT the man past take the book PASSIVE

The surface structures of sentences 17 and 18 look rather different, but from xvii and xviii it is apparent that the difference results from the fact that 18 contains a reflex of the **PASSIVE** in xviii. All of the other changes in 17 and 18 are equally automatic consequences of the deep structures xvii and xviii. The English verbal element *do* quite often occurs in surface structures for such reasons as those just outlined and is often nothing more than a reflex of some aspect of deep structure, as in sentences **19–22**:

19 John didn't go.
20 Did John go?
21 John did go!
22 I went and John did too.

In these sentences the *do* carries the tense element of the deep structure, but for varying reasons: because of the deep *NOT* in xix, the deep *QUESTION* in xx, the deep *EMPHATIC* in xxi, and those rules of anaphora that have to do with the permissible repetition of verbs within a sentence in xxii:

xix NOT John past go
xx QUESTION John past go
xxi EMPHATIC John past go
xxii I past go and John past go too

Not all instances of *do* come from such sources as these—the *do* of 23 does not, nor does the second *do* of 24, but the first *do* of 24 comes from deep *EMPHATIC:*

23 I do my homework at home.
24 I do do my homework at home.

These examples provide good illustrations of a transformation that adds to the surface structure of a sentence an element not present in the deep structure. They also explain just how the sentences must be interpreted to "make sense."

Three superficially different question patterns are illustrated by sentences 25, 26, and 27:

25 Did the man take the book?
26 Who took the book?
27 What took the book?

These three sentences have the following deep structures:

xxv QUESTION the man past take the book
xxvi QUESTION SOMEONE past take the book
xxvii QUESTION SOMETHING past take the book

Sentence 25 is a simple "yes-no" question in that it is answerable either affirmatively or negatively, whereas sentences 26 and 27 cannot be answered so simply. From xxv it is apparent that there is no element in the deep structure to be questioned, so the *QUESTION* element must be attached to the total proposition. In xxvi and xxvii, however, there are dummy elements in the deep structure to which *QUESTION* may be properly attached, so *QUESTION SOMEONE* in xxvi and *QUESTION SOMETHING* in xxvii produce

Who? and *What?* respectively in the surface structures 26 and 27. Whereas *SOMEONE, SOMETHING,* and *SOMENOUN* are dummy elements which trigger certain transformations, *someone* and *something* are lexical items—like *book* and *take*—which are inserted into deep structures. This difference accounts for the differences in meaning among such sentences as *Who took the book? (QUESTION SOMEONE ...), Did someone take the book? (QUESTION someone ...),* and *Someone took the book. (Someone ...).*

Sentence 28 is still more complicated than any of the preceding sentences:

28 What was taken?
xxviii QUESTION SOMENOUN past take SOMETHING PASSIVE

In order to understand sentence 28 one must understand all of the following points, each of which is represented in the deep structure xxviii. First of all, an unknown *SOMETHING* was taken and it was taken by an unknown *SOMENOUN.* Second, the person asking the question is more interested in what was taken than in who took it, so xxviii contains a *PASSIVE.* He also seeks information, so the *QUESTION* element is present. The passive transformation shifts the *SOMENOUN* into a *by SOMENOUN* phrase and a resultant deletion. This transformation does not affect the *QUESTION* and *SOMETHING* elements, which then undergo the additional transformations resulting in *What?* The total process may be characterized somewhat as follows:

[Initial string: deep structure]
xxviii QUESTION SOMENOUN past take SOMETHING PASSIVE
[Passive transformation: rearrangement and addition of *be en*]
QUESTION SOMETHING past be en take by SOMENOUN
[Deletion transformation]
QUESTION SOMETHING past be en take
[Question transformation: rearrangement]
past be SOMETHING en take
[wh- transformation]
what past be en take

> [Affix transformation: rearrangement]
> what be past take en
> [Final sentence: surface structure]
> **28** What was taken?

An understanding of **28** requires one to be aware of the content of **xxviii**. There are only three words in **28**, but these words are the reflexes of a considerable deep structure which triggers the process outlined above and which is partly characterized in **xxviii**.

It is possible to go much further with this type of analysis in order to reveal just what must be understood to be in the deep structure of any sentence. Some example sentences follow to show the considerable variety of deep structures that occur in English.

Sentence **29** is a command or imperative sentence:

> **29** Take the book!
> **xxix** IMPERATIVE you present will take the book

Sentence **29** is such a sentence because it has the ***IMPERATIVE*** element, or formative, in its deep structure, along with ***you pres-ent will***. This particular combination results in a transformation that deletes all these elements to produce the surface structure. It is rather interesting that deep structure **xxix** justifies some of the traditional claims about imperative sentences having a "***you*** understood" in them. It also accounts for such a possibility in English as sentence **30**:

> **30** Take the book, will you!

It should be noted that *will* (or *won't*) is the only possible modal verb that can accompany an English imperative and that *you* is the only possible pronoun. The ungrammaticality of **31** and **32** is all too obvious to a native speaker of English:

> **31** °Take the book, can you!
> **32** °Take the book, will he!

Sentences **33** and **34** show some interesting facts about how pronouns are understood:

> **33** The man hurt himself.
> **xxxiii** the man[1] past hurt the man[1]

34 The man hurt him.

xxxiv the man[1] past hurt the man[2] PRONOMINALIZA-
TION

Both sentences contain transitive verbs and objects, but the objects reveal that different people suffered the hurt. *Him* and *himself* are pronouns and substitute for noun phrases. In xxxiii the noun phrase for which *himself* substitutes is *the man[1];* the superscript shows that it is identical with the noun phrase that is the sentence subject, also *the man[1].* The *him* in 33 results from a constraint in English that requires the use of a substitute, and *self* results from the identity of the referents. In 34 the *him* results from a pronominalization of *the man[2]* (or a human male) not identical with *the man[1].* We understand 33 to be about one man and the verb to be reflexive, whereas we understand 34 to be about two men (or one man and a second human male).

Sentence 35 illustrates how modifiers of nouns must be understood:

35 The young man took the book.

xxxv the man[1] (the man[1] past young) past take
the book

The young man in 35 means *The man was young* and xxxv indicates just such a deep structure for 35. The derivation of sentence 35 from xxxv also illustrates the important notion of recursiveness or embedding. Sentence 35 comes from two deep sentences, one of which is embedded in the other. The grammatical model offers an explanation, therefore, of how many of the sentences we use and understand may be paraphrased by several other sentences, each of which expresses only a part of the original sentence. It also offers an explanation of how we can always increase the length of any sentence by adding on a part with a meaning that could be expressed in a very simple sentence.

Sentences 36–39 are interesting because, like sentence 35, they are all *complex* in their deep structures—that is, derived from more than one sentence—though *simple* in their surface structures, in the usual terminology of traditional grammar:

36 I wanted the boy to go.

xxxvi I past want IT (the boy past go)

37	I asked the boy to go.
xxxvii	I past ask the boy[1] IT (the boy[1] past go)
38	I wanted the boy to be heard.
xxxviii	I past want IT (SOMEONE past hear the boy PASSIVE)
39	I took the boy to be examined.
xxxix	I past take the boy[1] (SOMEONE past examine the boy[1] PASSIVE)

A correct understanding of sentences **36** and **39** does not make the boy the same kind of "object" of the verb in each case, because there is an obvious difference between "taking" *the boy* on the one hand in **39** and "wanting" something *(IT)* on the other in **36**. In sentences **36** and **38** *the boy* is not the deep object of *wanted*. In **36** *the boy* is actually the deep subject of the verb *go*, and in **38** *the boy* is the deep object of the verb *hear*. In each case the noun phrase and the verb are part of the structure of an embedded sentence that as a whole functions as the deep object of *want*. It is relationships such as these which the deep structures **xxxvi–xxxix** bring out: it is possible to understand sentences **36–39** only insofar as one can project the readings of **xxxvi–xxxix** into those sentences.

Sentences **40** and **41** are not unlike sentences **36–39** in the problems they raise:

40	The man is difficult to please.
xl	SOMETHING (SOMENOUN present please the man) present difficult
41	The man is ready to please.
xli	the man[1] present ready (the man[1] present please SOMEONE)

Superficially, both **40** and **41** appear to have the same structure and to have identical problems in interpretation. But the deep structures **xl** and **xli** are quite different, and **40** and **41** can be understood properly only if these underlying differences are grasped.

It must be emphasized that the process of analysis we have been discussing is not put forward as a model of an actual psychological process that listeners or readers go through in order to understand sentences. Such an *analytic process* is sometimes referred to as "analysis by synthesis," and while it is a rather attractive notion because it can be formalized quite easily, it nevertheless seems unrealistic because of the "real" time it would require to operate. That any comprehender operates in this way is extremely unlikely. A model of the actual process of comprehension must somehow incorporate just the grammatical facts illustrated above, however, and must somehow explain the fact that sentences appear to be interpreted in the manner shown above. The actual model presented in this chapter is what is called a "competence" model, not a "performance" model. It claims to do no more than to show *what* must be explained in a performance model, not *how* it must be explained. Many investigators have tried to use the model as a performance model, in investigating, for example, how long it takes subjects to perform certain linguistic tasks with "simple" sentences, "complex" sentences, "kernel" sentences, and so on. That the results of such experiments have usually been inconclusive is not surprising, in view of the very nature of the theory on which they were based, which makes no claims about actual linguistic performance.

Mature language users can detect ambiguous sentences, deviant sentences, and ungrammatical sentences. Actually, ambiguous sentences are not usually taken to be ambiguous on first hearing or reading, just as an ambiguous figure, such as the Necker cube below, is seen in one way at first glance. The ambiguity of the figure is revealed only on further inspection. Even after the ambiguity of the cube is perceived, both forms cannot be perceived simultaneously: the cube must assume one form or the other at any particular moment, even though these moments may be very short and perception may vacillate quickly from one form to the other.

Necker cube

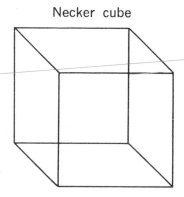

Sentences **42, 43,** and **44** may not be regarded as ambiguous on first reading, because they will each be assigned a single deep structure immediately:

42   He greeted the lady with a smile.
43   He likes good food and wine.
44   An old book salesman came.

A second reading of these sentences may reveal that each is ambiguous, particularly when that sentence is placed in an entirely different context from the first context in which it was met and in which it was interpreted.

Sentences **42, 43,** and **44** are ambiguous because each actually can be assigned at least two different deep structures as follows:

xliia   he past greet the lady[1] (the lady[1] past have a smile)
xliib   he[1] past greet the lady (he[1] past have a smile)
xliiia   he[1] present like food[1] (the food[1] present good): he[1] present like wine
xliiib   he[1] present like food[1] (the food[1] present good): he[1] present like wine[1] (the wine[1] present good)
xliva   a man[1] (the man[1] past sell books[1] [the books[1] past old]) past come
xlivb   a man[1] (the man[1] past sell books) (the man[1] past old) past come

In each case, two different deep structures undergo a series of transformations, and the transformational processes produce identical surface structures. This single surface structure is consequently ambiguous, because it has two possible interpretations, one for each of the deep structures. Sentence **42** can be read with either *he* or *the lady* doing the smiling, sentence **43** can be read so that *he* likes *good food* and *good wine* or he likes *good food* and *wine* of any quality, and sentence **44** can be read so that the *salesman* sells *old books* or that he is *old* and sells *books* which themselves may or may not be old. Any particular reading requires the assignment of one deep structure or the other; just as it is impossible to see the Necker cube in both its possibilities concurrently, so it is impossible to assign each of sentences **42, 43,** and **44** both of their readings simultaneously. It is necessary to assign one reading or the other, even though it is quite possible to switch extremely rapidly from one reading to the other, just as it is possible to switch rapidly from one interpretation of the cube to the other.

Any adequate theory of comprehension must deal satisfactorily with the problems of interpretation that ambiguous sentences create. It must employ devices for handling ambiguity that are not *ad hoc*—that is, devices required elsewhere in the grammar. It must also explain why in practice ambiguous sentences are not usually discovered to be ambiguous on first reading. Such a theory must also account for the fact that certain "sentences" cannot be given any reading at all, or only a forced reading. It is, for example, impossible to give **45** any kind of reading at all:

45 *Will come yesterday he.

Example **45** cannot be given a reading, because it is impossible to project a deep structure for this collection of words. Since there is no deep structure for **45,** the collection of words is meaningless. On the other hand "sentence" **46** may be given some kind of reading, but only by projecting the kind of reading normally given to a sentence like **47,** in which the adverbial time-word and the tense of the verb do not conflict as they do in **46:**

46 He will come yesterday.
47 He will come tomorrow.

Sentence **47** is an unremarkable sentence, whereas "sentence" **46** is remarkable: it is the kind of "sentence" that appears in contexts where so-called "figurative" language is appropriate. Indeed, it might prove a fruitful hypothesis to consider that the sentences of figurative language are figurative for the very reason that they break some of the minor constraints of the language. The breaking of these constraints does not prevent such "sentences" from being interpreted on the same basis as sentences which do not break them, but it marks the sentences as non-normative. Collections of words such as **45,** which break too many constraints or break major ones, cannot have any kind of deep structure projected for them, so they are not interpretable at all. Again, an adequate theory of comprehension must offer a satisfactory explanation for the different reactions one has to **45, 46,** and **47.** Such a theory must also allow one to say something about the different reactions that speakers of English have to **48–51:**

48   The boy liked the dog.
49   They are eating apples.
50   Anyone lived in a pretty how town.
51   *Shall go he to is.

In these examples **48** may be said to be grammatical, **49** to be ambiguous, **50** to be deviant, and **51** to be ungrammatical. The theory outlined in this chapter suffices to explain all of these examples, and no additional grammatical apparatus is required for **49** through **51** that was not required to account for sentences like **48.**

These last few examples show some of the essential characteristics of poetic language. The language of poetry is deviant, in the sense that it varies from a norm of some kind and not in any pejorative sense; it cannot stray too far from the norm, of course, or the result is nonsense. The deviance may be of various kinds: obviously, poetic meter and such devices as onomatopoeia and alliteration result from phonological deviance, and metaphor arises from grammatical and semantic deviance. Poetic language is not something mysterious or something that should not be subject to close examination for fear of spoiling it. Poetic language is a variation of normal language. To understand how people understand the language of poetry, it is necessary to know how that language varies from normal language. There is more to a total understanding of a poem than understanding how the linguistic part of the content works, of course, but one cannot ignore that part if one wants to know how poetry gains its total effect. Those critics who insist on a close examination of poetic texts are likely to gain much from the insights of generative-transformational grammar.

In the discussion of sentences in this chapter, we have seen that for a sentence to make sense it must have a deep structure, so that it conforms to the grammar of the language. Another way of saying this is that for a set of words to *be* a sentence, it must have a deep structure. A set of words that has no deep structure is not a sentence. A sentence by definition, then, must have grammatical meaning. The meaning of any sentence also depends to some extent on its lexical items, but without a deep structure these lexical items cannot make sense. It is totally inadequate to define the meaning of a sentence as simply a fusion, of some mysterious sort, of the meanings of the lexical items. We must seek to understand what is meant by fusion and try to characterize the process as explicitly as possible. We must also seek to give precise definitions to such terms as the "main idea" of a sentence if we propose that children read certain sentences to "get the main idea."

Even the very "simple" sentences of beginning reading texts can profitably be analyzed using the grammatical approach sketched in this chapter. Two sentences such as

Here is something pretty. Something pretty for you and me.

which follow each other in one primer may be very short and contain highly frequent words, but grammatically they are not easy to understand. The first sentence contains an inversion of *here* and *something* and is derived from two sentences, *Something is here* and *Something is pretty.* The second sentence, a fragment in traditional terminology, can be understood only if *Here is* is supplied to make the whole sentence read *Here is something pretty for you and me.* It also contains the same problem as the first with *something* and *pretty* and the additional *for you and (for) me* relationship to *something.* Superficially, these two sentences may look easy, but this appearance is deceptive. Such sentences may well create comprehension problems for children, particularly when their surface structures, as in the second example, are also relatively infrequent in comparison with the other surface structures in the same text. Existing measures of sentence complexity must be used with caution, for they do not always adequately reveal the full complexity of certain sentences they treat as simple.

In addition to their interest in the complex internal structures of sentences, some linguists have shown an interest in the external relationships of sentences to each other in larger units such as paragraphs and stories.

Interpreting utterances, both spoken and written, that are larger than the sentence involves reacting to the signals that are in the text but distributed over several utterances or sentences rather than within a particular utterance or sentence. Here an important distinction must be made between the interpretation of spoken utterances, as in a dialogue, and the interpretation of written sentences organized into paragraphs and larger expository and narrative works. In a dialogue the listener has the opportunity to ask for clarification when he does not understand something, and the utterances he must comprehend are usually less complex than those of written discourse. Dialogue is also likely to contain performance characteristics such as mazes, repetitions, switches, hesitations, incompletions, and so on. Some of these performance characteristics result from the fact that human beings have certain memory limitations (Miller, 1956). Others are the result of the use of language for "phatic communion" —that is, to establish and maintain communication between speakers and to keep the channels of communication open for use when needed, rather than to say anything specific (Malinowski, 1923). Still others are the result of the particular interpersonal opportunities that dialogue and conversation provide. In other words, the performance characteristics are of a particular kind, to which the child has always been accustomed even before he began to read. It was just such language that provided him with the data he needed to acquire his linguistic competence. In reading, on the other hand, there are new and different performance variables, which may cause students difficulties in learning to read. Some of these variables have to do with the deliberately controlled nature of written communication, and others have to do with the different ways in which sentences are connected to each other. Such differences can easily be discovered if, on the one hand, one attempts to edit for publication an impromptu talk or if, on the other hand, one attempts to read a formal paper in a very formal manner to a small, informal group.

On the whole, generative-transformational grammarians have not concerned themselves with structures larger than the sentence, except perhaps insofar as they have had to deal with the troublesome problem of sentence compounding. One generative-transformational grammarian, Postal (1966, pp. 198–99), has denied the need to become involved in what he calls "discourse contexts" in order to explain such matters as pronominalization, as in *She dances well.* However, there do appear to be higher level structures in discourse than those of the sentence, and Pike (1964), Becker (1965), and others have concerned themselves with a search for structural signals beyond the sentence.

Becker has pointed out that the units traditionally called paragraphs do have some linguistic reality, in expository prose at least, and that this reality does not depend solely on the artifact of indentation. There are definite places in such prose where both grammatical and lexical changes co-occur—for example, changes in tense or aspect and changes in vocabulary—and such change-points appear to mark the boundaries of paragraphs. It is obvious too that we can all distinguish sets of random sentences from sets of related sentences and perceive different types of relationships within the latter sets. Some such relationships have to do with determiner sequences such as *a* followed by *the;* with deictics such as *this* and *that;* with pronominal sequences such as *John-he* and *Mary-she;* with substitutes such as *do* and *so;* with sequencing or contrasting words such as *first, second, then, after, therefore,* and *however;* with ellipses, comparisons, and various subtle types of anaphora. All of these devices are used in speaking, but in writing they are used more deliberately, in a much more controlled manner. The reader must learn to react to the different distribution of such signals and, therefore, to rather different demands of interpretation and understanding. In more elaborate prose that makes use of extensive parallelisms, balanced sentences, and intricate word patterning, the demands on the neophyte reader will be even greater.

The following paragraph taken from a story in a fifth-grade book illustrates just a few of the devices mentioned above:

> He studied the boys in the town where he lived to determine which would be the best sorcerer's apprentice. He invited many of them to his house for interviews. Finally he decided upon a lad named Hans. Hans seemed a clever lad and eager to learn, and besides his father was willing to pay a sum of money for him to live with Frankel and learn the trade of sorcery.

The *he* of the first line actually refers back to a noun phrase *Frankel,* in the previous paragraph. Until *Hans* is mentioned all the third person singular *him* references are to *Frankel,* but afterward they are to *Hans.* There are other relationships too: the tense is consistently past; *them* refers back to *boys; finally, and,* and *besides* give order and continuity; certain collocations occur—that is, word sets with internal semantic relationships—particularly the collocation *boy, lad, apprentice, learn,* and *trade.*

As yet there is little information available on how sentences relate to each other, but linguists are greatly interested in the problem.

Some linguists attempt to propose solutions that set up structures beyond the sentence, whereas others prefer to set up sentence-interpreting schema that do not require such structures. Both groups are referring to basically the same set of problems, however, and although the proposed solutions may differ as a result of different theoretical orientations, the fact that the problems are being considered is a noteworthy development in current linguistics and one that is sure to have its consequences for the teaching of reading.

CHAPTER SIX

Meaning

The usual approach that reading researchers and teachers have taken in trying to understand how the reader comprehends a sentence is to regard the meaning of a sentence as basically a combination of the meanings of the individual words in it; the reader discovers the meaning of the total sentence by fusing the meanings of its parts. In other words, the task in reading and also apparently in aural comprehension is to decide on the meaning of each word in a sentence in some kind of linear order and then combine these meanings in the unique way that "makes sense" out of all the different meanings. In no way can the process be a passive one, because words have different meanings and these require the processer to make decisions about the precise meaning a word must have in a particular context; relatively little attention is ever focused on this decision-making process, however, and on the constraints that must operate within it. As we saw in the previous chapter, such a characterization of how sentences achieve their meanings or of the process of "getting meaning from the printed page" is grossly inadequate; nevertheless it prevails. Largely as a result of recent advances in linguistics and semantics, it is now possible to offer a more adequate characterization of how sentences achieve their meanings and of the significant components in the processing operation.

We saw in the last chapter that part of the inadequacy of many existing characterizations of the meaning in sentences resides in an almost total disregard of their syntactic structures. The structural linguists paid very serious attention to such linguistic concepts as the form classes of words, possible word orders, and the constituent structures of sentences in their discussions of meaning. They did not use meaning in their analytical processes, except differential meaning (sameness or difference) because, given the goal of explaining how meaning was achieved in sentences, they wanted to avoid the circularity that would result if they used meaning in their procedures.

Linguists such as Fries (1945, Chapter 4) emphasized the critical distinction between lexical and grammatical words that structural linguists had to observe for a language such as English. The first group, the lexical words, are the *content* words of the language. Such words make reference to the "things," "actions," and "qualities" in the "real" world. The "thing" words are very much the same as the traditional grammarian's "noun" class—words like *dog, bread,* and *water,* on the one hand, with rather concrete meanings, and *hope, transformation,* and *iniquity,* on the other, with abstract meanings. The "action" words are very much the same as the traditional grammarian's "verb" class. Again, this class has many different kinds of members, such as *jump, hope,* and *enhance.* The "quality" words are very much the same as the traditional grammarian's "adjective" class, words such as *old, beautiful,* and *friendly.* The grammatical words do not refer to the "real" world in the same way as the lexical words; they are "function" words such as *may, the, if,* and *be* or "substitute" words such as *do, so,* and *one.* The grammatical words generally provide the framework or structures for the lexical words.

A close examination of sentences 1 and 2 indicates how such a distinction between lexical and grammatical words operates in English:

1 The boy will go to the zoo in a car.
2 Our friends are taking courses at the university.

Sentence 1 contains ten words of which four are lexical words as shown in **ia**:

ia —— boy —— go —— —— zoo —— —— car.

On the other hand, **ib** shows the grammatical words in sentence 1:

    ib   The —— will —— to the —— in a ——.

The lexical content of sentence 2 is shown in **iia** and the grammatical content in **iib**:

    iia   —— friend —— —— tak(e) —— course —— —— —— university.

    iib   Our ——s are ——ing ——s at the ——.

There is one difference that should be noted between **ia** and **ib** on the one hand and **iia** and **iib** on the other. The noun ending *-s* and the verb ending *-ing* are mapped with the grammatical content of sentence 2 rather than with the lexical content. Actually there appears to be little reason to map these elements in one of these dimensions rather than the other, because the lexical-grammatical distinction is not clear-cut. Recent work in linguistics shows that the distinction cannot be very clear and that it most certainly cannot be made at the level of surface structure, as in these examples. In spite of this theoretical weakness, however, the distinction has considerable value in that it allows us to gain some fundamental insights into a variety of problems. It is possible, for example, to insert many different lexical items into the "frame" which **ib** provides and thereby create sentences, such as 3, 4, and 5:

    3   The man will cruise to the island in a yacht.
    4   The girl will come to the party in a taxi.
    5   The explorer will descend to the ocean floor in a submarine.

The distinction also helps us to understand how such a poem as "Jabberwocky" can fill our heads with meaningless ideas, just as Alice's was when she first heard it from Humpty Dumpty. It also has proved to be a very teachable distinction in linguistics, and nonsense sentences such as 6 and 7 have often been used to point out the differences between grammatical structure and lexical meaning:

    6   The moops oogled the wibbly wuggles.
    7   All the boakness was gibbled up.

The lexical-grammatical distinction is obviously a useful one, particularly in that it stresses the importance of the grammatical meanings in sentences.

If one wishes to propose that the meaning of a sentence results from a process of fusion, he must account for the fact that both lexical and grammatical words must be fused and that they are classes of words with very different characteristics. As we have seen, however, the fusion metaphor itself is a poor and unrevealing one in that it short circuits the process of explaining exactly what happens when someone understands a sentence. The concern should be with exactly what factors are involved in fusion and why fusion occurs on some occasions but not on others. Such problems deserve serious consideration. The structural linguist who describes the grammatical elements and patterns of English acknowledges the fact that these provide the necessary framework for the lexical content of English. He tries to isolate some of the basic components that must form part of a model of comprehension, and he raises serious questions about the nature and universality of these components and even about his own analytical techniques and assumptions. The linguist attempts, therefore, to ask the right questions about what the various components of sentences must be if those sentences are to be comprehensible. For example, the structural linguist tries to characterize the permissible grammatical patterns and to discover where lexical items may be entered into these patterns to make meaningful sentences. A combination of an English pattern and suitable English lexical items will result in a meaningful English sentence. A non-English pattern or incorrectly chosen lexical items will, on the other hand, result at best in a deviant sentence, at worst in a completely incomprehensible sentence.

A very different approach to the problem of meaning, or to the control of meaning in reading texts, relies on word and structure frequency counts. The assumptions behind such an approach vary from user to user. For example, it is sometimes assumed that the meaning burden of a passage is lightened if high frequency words are substituted for low frequency words or high frequency structures for low frequency ones, because high frequency is taken to be closely related to familiarity and therefore to ease of comprehension. Other times frequency is tied to regularity, and the selection of words and structures is based not only on whether they are frequent but also on the extent to which they follow the regular productive patterns, for example, in inflection and in spelling. It is a well-known fact that in English many irregular forms occur very frequently, both spellings such as *of, were,* and *one* and grammatical forms such as *men, children, has,* and *are.* Hall (1964), for example, criticizes reading texts as follows: "Such texts ... jumble together, haphazardly, spellings which are regular (*can* or *met*), semi-irregular (*Pete, meat; bear, bare*) and quite irregular (*laugh, money*)" (p. 429). The criticism has considerable validity, even though the regularity principle that Hall is using is not fully explicit, because it could be argued that *Pete* is every bit as regular as *met* in its spelling.

Frequency is also an important factor to be considered in introducing new words into beginning reading texts and in controlling the repetition of such words. "New" in this sense of course means being presented visually for the first time; they are certainly not new aurally. Frequency is also important to anyone interested in making various kinds of statistically based orthographic, grammatical, and lexical approximations to English, in using "cloze" procedures which rely on omitting every *n*th word, and in any kind of lexical glossing, such as dictionary-making.

The subject of word frequency counts is a fascinating one for some researchers. There are many possibilities to count and compute, there is much research that apparently should be done, and there are many results that could be useful. The real problem is knowing just what is worth doing and how important frequency is in language. That certain linguistic items occur more frequently than others in any language is obvious. What is not so obvious is the significance of that observation—for example, in helping one decide how to control such items in texts, how to grade linguistic materials, or how to deal with the combinatorial frequencies of words as well as with their individual frequencies. On the whole, most linguists have shown little concern with such matters as frequency except when they have found insights from related disciplines, such as the communication sciences, to be valuable in their work. Fries and Traver (1950) gave considerable attention to word lists, their bases, and particularly to their usefulness in language instruction. Their book *English Word Lists* discusses some of the inadequacies of existing lists and indicates several areas in which such lists could be improved, such as in treating colloquial English, age grading, derivational patterning, compounding, and functional shifting.

Any examination of word lists shows that they usually do not deal very satisfactorily with the important matters of how words are actually used in different contexts, their varying grammatical uses, and homonymity. Part of the difficulty, of course, arises from the fact that it is almost impossible to decide on suitable criteria for defining the term *word* in English—that is, for saying what is to be counted as one word and what as two or more words. Is *houseboat* one word, or is it two because of the existence of such a combination as *house party*? Is *hope* in *I hope* a different word from *hope* in *the hope*? Is *a* a different word from *an,* is *man* a different word from *men,* and is *has* a different word from *have*? How many words are there in each of the triplets *good, better,* and *best* and *drink, drank,* and *drunk*? Until such questions as these are answered on a principled basis, there seems to be little hope of producing word lists that take into account all the variables involved in word selection. The collocational characteristics of words—the ways particular words group with each other in sets—are also likely to be important, but almost nothing is known of this important variable.

In view of all the difficulties in compiling word lists and making frequency counts, it is not surprising that there has been some recent criticism of research procedures and of experimental and classifying techniques in both reading and psychology that depend on word lists. Since readability formulae such as the Dale-Chall and Flesch formulae rely heavily on word-frequency counts, any research based on the use of the formulae may be invalid if the counts themselves are inadequate. Word frequency has also been important in verbal learning studies even when these employ nonsense words, because such words must be related in some way to actually occurring words. Both *gleat* and *nglez* are nonsense words, but anyone literate in English knows that the first word is less "nonsensical" than the second because it is much more like a normal English word. At best, readability formulae and verbal learning studies based on present lists can offer only gross indications of readability and of verbal learning difficulties. Such must be the case as long as the lists continue to be based on *ad hoc* procedures and as long as many other linguistic variables are ignored.

Word frequencies are not the only frequencies that may be important in controlling the language used in reading texts. The frequencies of various grammatical structures are probably just as important. Since such structures are still more difficult to count, however, there has been less work on structure counts than on word counts. It is doubtful too that until recently enough was known about the important characteristics of grammatical structures to make any such accounts as revealing as they would need to be in order to be of use in constructing texts or investigating the development of syntactic ability in children. Given the present state of knowledge of English syntax, the frequency problem may well continue to be given little attention until solutions are found to more urgent problems relating to syntax and semantics and to the general form a linguistic description should take. The solutions of these problems would provide part of the theoretical base for controlling the frequencies of words and structures in texts, if such control still seems to be desirable after their solution.

The semantic differential described by Osgood, Suci, and Tannenbaum (1957) has also been much used in studies of meaning in reading. The differential has proved to be rather attractive to researchers for much the same reason that word frequency counts have been attractive: it is fairly easy to understand and to use. But it has serious limitations in that it is concerned with the connotational, impressionistic aspect of meaning, with the ways in which words and particularly various collocations of words affect or reveal one's behavior. Osgood, Suci, and Tannenbaum discovered three important and largely independent factors that help to define a semantic space into which words may be placed; these factors can be labeled an "evaluation" factor (good vs. bad), a "potency" factor (strong vs. weak), and an "activity" factor (fast vs. slow). Using these factors, they were then able to describe how groups of people and also particular individuals fitted certain words into this semantic space. The connection between this discovery and reading instruction, however, must be regarded as tenuous. If the words *dog, home,* and *doctor* do arouse different feelings in different people, that is certainly an interesting fact, but it is a fact about these people rather than about the language itself. It might be a fact that for speaker A these words all have pleasant connotations and that for B they all have unpleasant connotations; the critical problem, however, seems to be that of devising a semantic system which is not "differential"—that is, which is not concerned with plotting in some N-dimensions how a word differs in meaning for different people, but in devising a semantic system which characterizes the sameness of meaning the word has for all speakers of the language. Obviously this latter is a much more difficult and fundamentally more important task and will involve serious problems of definition and reference. It is far more important to know what speakers share in the semantic realm than what separates them, since any understanding of the latter is completely dependent on the former. The semantic differential itself may well require considerable revision, because as more becomes known of "normative" language use any theory of the "abnormative" will have to take into account this increase in knowledge.

Currently linguists are very much concerned with the problem of the relationship between syntax and semantics. This concern is not new; it was apparent among both traditional and structural grammarians. But the current effort is to show how the relationship of syntax and semantics may be described within a grammar of rules—that is, a grammar structured in the form discussed in the last chapter. A speaker's semantic knowledge of his language is no more random than his syntactic knowledge of it; therefore, it seems useful to consider the possibility of devising, for semantic knowledge, a set of rules similar in form to the set used to characterize syntactic knowledge. Exactly how such a set of rules should be formulated and exactly what it must explain are to a considerable extent uncertain. At the very least the rules must characterize some sort of norm, the kind of semantic knowledge that an ideal speaker of the language might be said to exhibit in an ideal set of circumstances—in short, his semantic competence. In this way the rules would characterize just that set of facts about English semantics that all speakers of English have internalized and can draw upon in interpreting words in novel combinations. When one hears or reads a new sentence, he makes sense out of that sentence by drawing on both his syntactic and his semantic knowledge. The semantic knowledge enables him to know what the individual words mean and how to put these meanings together so that they are compatible. To characterize this semantic knowledge, it seems desirable to postulate a set of rules that assigns a reading of some kind to each word. This reading would provide a statement of the essential semantic properties of the word, specifying these in accordance with a universal vocabulary of specifications, and a second statement of the combinatory possibilities of that word with others.

The two linguists who have been most closely concerned with formulating this kind of semantic approach are Katz and Fodor. Katz and Fodor (1963) have proposed a semantic theory that is closely related to the syntactic theory developed earlier by Chomsky. How it might characterize the basic semantic competence underlying comprehension may be shown somewhat as follows, using examples given by Nida (1964):

8 The man sat in the chair.
9 The man died in the chair.

In sentence 8 the correct semantic interpretation of *chair* requires that the word be assigned such semantic properties as "object," "human use," and perhaps something like "harmless." The exact properties required for the specification would be drawn from a set of such properties applicable to English. This set of properties itself would be a sub-set of a universal set of properties, one that would cover all languages. Sentence 9 might arouse a suspicion in the listener or reader that a "harmless" reading may not be appropriate, because the verb *died* appears in the sentence and the meanings projected for *died* and *chair* might well tend to create some uncertainty about the property "harmless" in the set of properties postulated for *chair*. Sentence 9 consequently has more likelihood of creating a problem in interpretation than sentence 8, but ordinarily it would not do so, for the normal reading would assign "harmless" rather than "harmful" to *chair;* given no more to interpret than the content of 9, the normal reaction is to accept the "harmless" reading.

In sentences 10 and 11 the faint potential ambiguity of 9 is no longer present: "harmful" now replaces "harmless" as the characteristic that must be projected for *chair:*

10 He died in the electric chair.
11 He died in the chair for his crime.

Electric in 10 and *for his crime* in 11 require that *chair* be given a different reading from *chair* in 8. These additions also help us to understand the difficulties encountered in the interpretation of 9.

In sentences **12** and **13** a reading for *chair* similar to that in **8** is apparently required:

12   He took the chair.
13   He accepted the chair.

The addition of *at the meeting* to **12**, however, would require a "role" rather than "object" characteristic for *chair,* as in **14**, just as would the addition of *at the university* to **13**, as in **15**:

14   He took the chair at the meeting.
15   He accepted the chair at the university.

Furthermore, *chair* in **14** would now require an additional "academic" characteristic.

This kind of approach to meaning requires the formulation of a sufficiently general set of semantic properties and a set of rules called projection rules to relate these to each other so that they can be used to describe some of the important *structured* properties of the meanings of individual words and of the meanings of the sets of words that are used in sentences. The resulting description could then be said to be a representation of the kind of system that speakers of a language have somehow internalized and that they draw upon in interpreting sentences. The claim is not that it is *the* system they have internalized but rather that it is a system that may usefully be said to resemble that system in various ways. As more and more becomes known about the rules governing semantic behavior, the system linguists devise to account for that behavior will change. What is really important is the basic principle involved in the total endeavor, the principle of trying to formalize in as explicit a way as possible the semantic knowledge that a mature listener or reader brings to his task of comprehension and that underlies his actual behavior in comprehension.

As we have previously indicated, a listener or reader does not gain the total meaning of a sentence by simply totaling up the meanings of the individual words in some kind of linear fashion as he might total up a grocery bill. Rather he combines a reading of the deep structure of the sentence with a reading of the meanings of the various lexical items and a projection of the readings of these lexical items to each other. In any particular sentence context, the projected meaning a word may have is derived in part from its intrinsic or dictionary meaning and in part from the context, so that, for example, in sentences 16 and 17 the total meaning of *fired* depends in part on the presence of *gun* in 16 and *manager* in 17:

16 The men fired the gun.
17 The men fired the manager.

An adequate statement about the fusion of meaning in sentences must be concerned not only with the deep syntactic structures of sentences but also with the semantic properties of the individual words and how these semantic properties are related in various ways as the words are arranged in sentences. Such a statement would also be normative in that it would concern ordinary, non-figurative language and not the language of literature nor of any other type of stylized language. The latter kind of language is best understood from the perspective of such a norm, since it seems obvious that a general ability to give correct syntactic and semantic interpretations to normal sentences and to normal language uses must underlie any specific ability to recognize linguistic nonsense or deviant language use. For example, this general ability allows one to interpret the deviant sentences of figurative and poetic language, as, for example, in sentences 18–22:

18 My dog passed away yesterday.
19 Salt is eating away my car's fenders.
20 All nature sleeps.
21 He sat in black despair.
22 The king was a lion in battle.

These sentences are recognized by speakers of English to be figurative—that is, somehow unusual and outside the everyday use of language. In sentence 18 the figurativeness arises from the use of the combination of *dog* and *passed away. Passed away* is a euphemism usually employed in reference to human beings and requires a subject with the property "human." *Dog* is assigned the property "non-human," however, so in this case *dog* must be considered to be endowed with some kind of humanity in order for the sentence to make sense. It is not too difficult for a reader to assign this property to *dog,* so that sentence 18 is allowable in a way that sentence 23 is not:

23   My cactus passed away yesterday.

Both human beings and dogs are "animate," but cactuses are "non-animate." A further restriction is therefore violated in 23, so that it is absurd whereas 18 is perhaps no more than sentimental. The verb *eat* in sentence 19 requires an animate subject, but *salt* is inanimate. The metaphoric quality of 19 results from relating this animate property of the verb to the subject *salt.* Much the same process can be observed in sentence 20, where *nature* is endowed with the animate property because of the need for *sleep* to have an animate subject. In sentence 21, *despair* obviously has the property of "abstractness" whereas *black* has one of "concrete." In sentence 22, there is a further instance of the "human" versus "non-human" juxtaposition, but in this case the *king* becomes endowed with the animal attributes of the *lion* because of the syntactic structure of the sentence. The preceding examples are deliberately simple, and they are not fully analyzed. They are discussed only to show how the theory can apply to figurative language as well as to normal language and to emphasize the point that such language can be understood only in terms of the "usual" or the "normative."

There may be some difficulties in conceiving of literary style and figurative language as "non-normative." Normal language must be made to appear rather flat and dull, and stylized language ornamental and somewhat deviant. But the approach outlined above has advantages. It allows for the postulation of a common set of rules to underlie both types of language, and it relates stylized language to normal language through a further set of rules of a very special kind. This second set would be useful in actually helping to define literature and style, and it would certainly provide a more precise analytical tool than such words as "flowing," "smooth," "harsh," "romantic," "tortuous," "paradoxical," and so on.

The above comments on figurative language would also indicate that students are in no position to appreciate the language of literature until they have a control of the normal language of everyday living, because literary appreciation depends on such control and cannot exist without it. Until students are able to listen to, read, and understand commonplace and prosaic utterances and writings, they have no hope of bringing any kind of linguistic competence to such expressions as *a grief ago, perform leisure, golf plays John,* and *misery loves company* (Chomsky, 1961). Such expressions will seem either incomprehensible or ridiculous to persons who have little or no facility with the syntactic and semantic structures of English because of their upbringing, lack of native ability, or inability to speak English like a native. Just as it is impossible to savor the phonological nuances of English poetry without a very complete familiarity with the system of English phonology, so it is impossible to appreciate the grammatical and semantic variations of poetry without an intuitive grasp of the grammatical and semantic systems. Undoubtedly many parts of the semantic system, and some parts of the syntactic and phonological systems, of standard English must be shared by speakers of any dialect of English, but a knowledge of . the particular combinations and variations which make up standard English comes only from learning standard English. Without such learning there is almost no hope of appreciating the literature written in that dialect. The truth of this can easily be discovered from one's experience with a foreign language. If one does not know Thai, he cannot distinguish between Thai poetry and Thai prose; if he knows only a little Thai, he cannot distinguish between good Thai poetry and bad Thai poetry; and until he really knows Thai like a cultured native Thai, he cannot distinguish between better and worse Thai poetry.

A knowledge of the semantic structure of English, or of any language, can be acquired only through use of that language. Although it is necessary to consider that there is a universal set of semantic properties of which a particular language uses a sub-set, the task for the learner of that language is one of determining just which sub-set he must learn. Fortunately, it is now possible to describe some of the properties of both the English sub-set and the universal set. As this description expands it will be possible to gain a more adequate understanding of just what is meant by meaning, of what processes must be accounted for in studies of how sentences achieve their meaning, and of how the process of comprehension might work.

At the present time the knowledge available for this kind of work in comprehension is severely limited. The discoveries made so far have been few and the new semantic theory discussed in this chapter is still in a primitive stage of development; in spite of this drawback, however, the new theory appears to be more promising than previous work on meaning. It must be fairly obvious that concerns with vocabulary development are misplaced when they are based on an inadequate notion of which characteristics of the total vocabulary of English are more important than others. Certainly frequency is an important factor in vocabulary development, but, just as certainly, it is neither the only nor the most important factor, and most certainly the available frequency counts are highly suspect. Vocabulary items should not be presented to children in a random manner, but neither should they be presented in a pseudo-scientific way based on inadequate frequency studies, poor semantic analyses, and randomly chosen contexts. As we have said, the semantic characteristics of a language can be learned only by using that language, but it should be possible to control and/or develop that use in a way that will produce maximal semantic development. Children do have difficulty in combining the individual meanings of words into meaningful patterns, a fact to which their "mistakes" readily testify. They also need help with some of the technical and special vocabulary of particular varieties of writing, in learning to understand such items as *yours truly, sic,* and *by these presents* and to react appropriately to the less redundant semantic structures used in writing.

Reading researchers and reading teachers will be the first to benefit from any increase in understanding of semantics, because they will then be in a much better position to understand one of the basic components of comprehension—the semantic component. This major component seems to comprise a set of dictionary-type readings for each word and a set of rules for combining these readings. Both sets apparently must conform to universal requirements: the first set may specify only certain universal properties, and the second set, sometimes called projection rules, must be fully explicit and of a universal type. Given such an understanding of semantics, workers in reading will have available to them a testable system for studying the semantic part of comprehension. It should allow them to avoid vague statements and at the same time should be testable, capable of refinement, and in accord with current hypotheses about language and language behavior.

CHAPTER SEVEN

The Spelling System of English

The alphabetic nature of the English writing system has been a source of both blessing and dismay to teachers of reading and writing. Alphabetic writing systems have advantages that non-alphabetic systems lack, as Gelb's book, A *Study of Writing* (1963), clearly reveals. In a system such as the Chinese, each word or morpheme—that is, each unit of meaning—is represented by its own sign; consequently, a learner must master a separate sign or combination of signs for each lexical item. There is no systematic connection between most written signs and the words with which they must be associated, just as there is no connection between a person's name and either his address or his telephone number. Learning a writing system of this kind is a formidable task because it places a tremendous burden on the memory. To become literate in such a system, one must learn many thousands of ideographs or logographs, some of which are ambiguous. In such circumstances mass literacy is very difficult to achieve, because learning all the symbols requires much time. Preliterate societies do not usually have the luxury of much free time available for the kind of study that mastery of such a system requires. Such societies are in need of the simplest and most economical writing systems, not the most laborious and complicated. Paradoxically, it is societies like those in North America that make available to their members the time needed for mastery of a writing system like Chinese, but it is just such societies that have alphabetic systems. Word writing systems are not only less economical than other systems but they are also older and may be said to represent an earlier stage in the development of writing systems.

The English writing system does employ some signs such as &, +, −, %, 1, 2, 3, and $3 \times 3 = 9$ that are not unlike the word signs used in Chinese, but they are few and almost always serve as a type of shorthand in one kind of technical writing or other. These signs also illustrate the one great advantage that such a system as the Chinese has: the signs can be "read," in the sense of pronounced, in any dialect of English and even in different languages. It is quite possible for speakers of two dialects of Chinese not to be able to understand each other's spoken language but to be able to communicate without difficulty in writing and to read the same text; they will, of course, pronounce that text quite differently and may even give its written symbols quite different grammatical arrangements. In the same way it is often possible for mathematicians who are monolingual speakers of different languages to "converse" with each other in print through their mathematical notations. To use an elementary example, an Englishman and a Frenchman would agree that $14 - 3 = 11$ is correct and $14 - 3 = 12$ is incorrect when these are presented on paper, even though they might not understand the spoken versions of the two equations.

In syllable systems, such as the Cherokee syllabary devised by Sequoia, each different syllable has its own symbol. The learning task and the memory burden are not so great with syllabaries as they are for word systems, because there are fewer different syllables in any language than there are different words, but the number is still considerable. Some languages lend themselves more easily to syllabaries and even to word writing systems than do others. For example, it is easier to devise a syllable system for a language in which syllables are of a regular and simple kind than for a language such as English, with its great variety of consonant clusters and its mixture of open and closed syllables. Likewise, it is easier to devise a word system for a language such as Chinese, with its massive preponderance of words composed of one morpheme, than for a language like Eskimo, with its extremely complicated word-building patterns. English is closer to Chinese than to

Eskimo in its word structures, but it is still sufficiently unlike Chinese to be easy to write in that system. Very little use is made of syllable writing devices in English, and what there is seems to be largely humorous: for example, I.O.U. (I owe you), O.I.C.U.2. (Oh, I see you too), and M.T.G.G. (Empty geegee = hungry horse). In contrast, Japanese is able to make extensive use of syllable writing conventions as a normal part of the writing system because of the nature of the syllabic patterns of spoken Japanese.

In the English writing system, basically an alphabetic one, each basic sound contrast, or phoneme, is usually represented by a single symbol. Note that it is necessary to say "usually." In all writing systems there appear to be some inconsistencies, for even the phonemic orthographies devised by structural linguists, the "purest" examples of alphabetic systems, have their arbitrary characteristics. In the English orthographic system, *cat* with its three contrasts /kæt/ is represented by three symbols, and *night* with its four contrasts /nayt/ is represented by five symbols. English does not have a set of one-to-one correspondences such that each contrast is represented by only one symbol and each symbol represents only one contrast. Linguists cannot even agree among themselves about the proper set of contrasts for English, so there seems to be little hope of establishing a definitive set of correspondences.

There are various reasons for the difficulties that linguists experience in devising an orthography for a language. One of them concerns the very concept of the phoneme itself—that is, the idea that any language utilizes a small set of significant contrastive sound units and that these contrastive units may be symbolized without a great deal of difficulty. Attempts have been made to devise various techniques for either discovering or postulating this set of contrasts, to make available to the linguist some kind of procedure that could be applied to the phonetic data of a language to produce just the right set of phonemes. For example, Pike's *Phonemics* (1947) outlines a set of procedures to follow in working out a phonemic system for a language so that an alphabetic writing system can be devised for it.

To work out the phonemic system of a language, a linguist must transcribe as many utterances of the language as are required to detect every different phonetic variant, until he reaches a point at which no new phonetic variants occur. To accomplish this, he must have proper training in phonetics—the science of describing and recording the sounds of speech. After he has recorded the utterances in a phonetic notation, employing brackets [ ], he attempts to discover which particular phonetic variants are related to each other as positional variants of what is basically a single contrast or phoneme (written between diagonal bars //). In English, for example, *pin* and *spin* have different *p*'s: aspirated in [p'm] and unaspirated in [spm]; *bat* and *bad* have different *a*'s: short in duration in [bæt] and longer in duration in [bæ·d]; and *geese* and *goose* have different *g*'s: "fronted" in [gɪⁱs] and "backed" in [gᵁᵘs]. These differences are *allophonic* in English—that is, predictable from the environments. Consequently, a *p*, or phoneme /p/, in a word must be pronounced [p'] if it is in initial position as in *pin* and as [p] if it follows *s* (/s/) as in *spin;* a vowel in front of a voiced consonant must be longer than the same vowel before a voiceless consonant, giving [æ] before /t/ in *bat* but [æ·] before /d/ in *bad;* and a *g* (/g/) before a front vowel in *geese* must be a fronted [g] and before a back vowel in *goose* must be a backed [g]. In English these are predictable differences in the phonemes /p/, /æ/, and /g/, and every native speaker makes the necessary variations unthinkingly. In fact he finds it almost impossible to do otherwise, and it is for just this reason that he is likely to carry over many of his English pronunciation habits in learning to speak a foreign language. The linguist has available a set of procedures which makes use of concepts such as phonetic similarity, complementary distribution, symmetrical patterning, and economy, in order to work out the phonemic system of a language. If the linguist believes that the system he works out for the language is in fact *the* system inherent in the language, then his procedures are discovery procedures and he has *discovered* the system; if, on the other hand, he believes the system he works out is no more than just a good working hypothesis, then he has *postulated* it for the language, and his procedures must be justified pragmatically, in terms of their usefulness.

Another approach to the same problems and one that is undoubtedly more powerful is discussed by Hockett in *A Course in Modern Linguistics* (1958), and by Gleason in *An Introduction to Descriptive Linguistics* (1961). Using this approach, a linguist looks for pairs of words that have a minimal difference in sound which also results in a difference in meaning, pairs such as *bat* and *pat, fail* and *veil, din* and *den,* and so on, in order to arrive at the minimal number of symbols it is necessary to have available in order to mark any two utterances which are distinguished by one phonemic contrast as differing by one symbol, distinguished by two contrasts by two symbols, and so on. Thus, in English, *bat* and *pat* may be symbolized as /bæt/ and /pæt/, *bat* and *pad* as /bæt/ and /pæd/, and *bat* and *pith* as /bæt/ and /piθ/. This approach avoids some of the difficulties described in the previous paragraph, but it is not fully comprehensive nor completely rigorous unless every possible contrast in the language can be established by reference to a minimal pair. It should be noted that even in such a thoroughly researched language as English this comprehensiveness does not appear to be attainable and some interesting *ad hoc* solutions result. For example, linguists do not agree on the phonemic interpretation of vowels in front of /r/ in English. *Bit* and *beat* show a contrast between /i/ and /iy/, just as *get* and *gate* show /e/ to contrast with /ey/. However, /i/ and /iy/ and /e/ and /ey/ do not contrast before /r/, so that one may equally well decide to transcribe *here* as either /hir/ or /hiyr/ and *pear* as either /per/ or /peyr/, and any decision to phonemicize in one way rather than in the other is quite arbitrary. Confronted with this particular phenomenon, known as neutralization, one linguist may employ a third symbol /ɪ/ for the vowel and write /hɪr/ rather than /hir/ or /hiyr/, whereas another may choose /hir/ rather than /hiyr/ on grounds of economy of symbol use or of phonetic similarity. No matter what the decision is, the result is a departure from a rigid application of the set of procedures for using minimal pairs to establish phonemic contrasts.

In the different approaches most difficulties can be resolved in one way or other, and any remaining differences in solutions among linguists are usually of the kind that can be related systematically, so that one linguist's /hir/ is another linguist's /hiyr/ and a third's /hɪr/, and one linguist's /bit/ is another's /bɪt/. A further principle in each approach would require that once a contrast in a particular environment has been assigned a symbol and identified in phonetic features, the same feature must be represented by that symbol in all other environments. Thus, if *sip* and *zip* are to be symbolized phonemically as /sip/ and /zip/ because they are a minimal pair showing an /s/-/z/ contrast, then *cats* and *dogs* must be symbolized as /kæts/ and /dɔgz/. The principle demands this solution even though the /s/-/z/ difference is completely predictable in the case of *cats* and *dogs* if the linguist is prepared to take grammatical and lexical information into account in his statements about phonology. However, many linguists have refused to allow any use of grammatical and lexical information in procedures for phonemicization. These linguists have insisted that statements about the phonemic system of a language make no reference to grammatical and lexical information, with the result that the phonemic statement will be quite autonomous, making reference only to phonetic information. This point of view about phonemic systems has been dominant in American linguistics until very recently and has been behind nearly all work conducted so far into phoneme-grapheme correspondences.

One phonemic system for English that has resulted from the principles just described and some common variants of the symbols used in that system are given in Table I, together with many of the graphemic correspondences of the phonemes. Table I is therefore a table of sound-spelling, or phoneme-grapheme, correspondences. The table will not be correct in all details for all dialects of English, but a speaker of any dialect may use it to gain some idea of the major spelling patterns of English.

Table 1   English Phoneme-Grapheme Correspondences

I. *Consonants*

	Initial	Medial	Final
p	*p*in	sli*pp*er, pi*p*er	ni*p*
t	*t*in	si*tt*er, Pe*t*er, deb*t*or	fi*t*, recei*pt*, deb*t*
č or tʃ	*ch*in, *c*ello	ca*tch*er, rap*t*ure	ca*tch*, ri*ch*
k	*c*an, *k*itten, *ch*asm, *q*uick	pa*ck*er, ba*k*er, li*qu*or	sa*ck*, brea*k*, opa*que*
b	*b*in	ru*bb*er, tu*b*a	ni*b*
d	*d*in	la*dd*er, so*d*a	pa*d*, shou*ld*
ǰ or dʒ	*j*ug, *g*entle	le*dg*er, sol*di*er, wa*g*er	ba*dge*, ra*ge*
g	*g*o, *gh*etto	bi*gg*er, ti*g*er	ra*g*

f	*f*in, *ph*oto	ba*ff*le, tou*gh*er, si*ph*on, hei*f*er	li*f*e, rou*gh*, cu*ff*
θ	*th*in	e*th*er	pa*th*
s	*s*in, p*s*alm, *c*enter, *sc*ience	pa*ss*er, ra*c*er	pa*ss*, thi*s*
š or ʃ	*sh*in, *s*ure	sma*sh*er, spe*ci*ous, omni*sci*ent, o*cea*n, pa*ssi*on, na*ti*on	la*sh*
v	*v*ein	fli*vv*er, mo*v*er	wa*v*e
ð	*th*en	*c*i*th*er	ba*th*e
z	*Z*en	lo*s*er, bla*z*er, no*zz*le	rou*s*e, dog*s*, ja*zz*
ž or ʒ	——	mea*s*ure, a*z*ure, delu*s*ion	——
m	*m*an	ha*mm*er, ta*m*er, co*mb*er	ha*m*, autu*m*n, to*mb*
n	*n*ip, *kn*it, g*n*aw	si*nn*er, fi*n*er	pi*n*, si*gn*
ŋ	——	si*ng*er, dri*n*k	si*ng*
r	*r*ed, *wr*eck, *rh*etoric	bea*r*er, hu*rr*y	he*r*, bu*rr*
l	*l*ong	fi*ll*ing, sai*l*or	ha*ll*, meta*l*
y	*y*et	Saw*y*er	sa*y*
h	*h*ot, w*h*o	a*h*ead	——
w	*w*et, (*wh*ere)	sho*w*er	co*w*

II. *Vowels*

iy or i	b*ea*t, b*ee*t, rec*ei*ve, rec*ei*pt, gr*ie*ve, bel*ie*f, ma*ch*ine, sk*i*, qu*ay*, k*ey*, sc*e*ne, b*e*, p*eo*ple, C*ae*sar, happ*y*
i or ɪ	b*i*t, bu*i*ld, h*y*mn, b*u*sy, w*o*men, g*i*ve, *E*ngland
ey or e	b*ai*t, m*a*te, m*ay*, m*ai*d, gr*ey*, str*ai*ght, g*au*ge, br*ea*k, w*ei*gh, r*ei*n
e or ɛ	b*e*t, h*ea*d, s*ai*d, fr*ie*nd, l*ei*sure, m*a*ny, l*eo*pard
æ	b*a*t, l*au*gh, h*a*ve
uw or u	b*oo*t, l*u*te, bl*ue*, fl*ew*, l*o*se, l*oo*se, fl*u*, fr*ui*t, thr*ou*gh, wh*o*, can*oe*

yuw or yu	beauty, mule, few, you, view
u or ʊ	good, bull, wolf, should
ow or o	boat, vote, show, shoulder, beau, though, sew, yeoman, go, woe
ɔ	dog, bought, taught, taut, law, broad, water, walk
a	not
ay or ai	bite, fight, my, flies, buy, bind, guile, height, stein, eye, aisle
ah	father, ah, mirage
aw or au	about, plow, bough
ɔy	Boyd, noise, adroit
⎰ ə¹ or ʌ¹	but, blood, enough, won, love
⎱ ə²	butter, bottle, metal, pleasure, soda, sailor, cherub, barrel, carrot, spirit, ocean
ar	cart, heart
er	pair, pare, pear, there
ir	ear, here, beer
ɔr	oar, floor, war, pour, hoarse, horse, bore
ur	poor
yur	pure, Muir
ər¹	her, shirt, word, lurk, pearl, Byrd, journal

¹ stressed
² unstressed

The symbols used in Table I for the phonemes have a deliberate mnemonic value in that they are as close to regular English spelling as possible. How close they actually do come to that spelling may be gauged from the following sentences, which are given in both their orthographic and phonemic representations. The suprasegmental phonemes (the contrasts of pitch, pause, and stress) are omitted from the phonemic transcriptions.

1   The cat sat on the mat.
i   /ðə kæt sæt ɔn ðə mæt/
2   Have you had enough?
ii   /hæv yuw hæd ənəf/
3   Please don't wait under the trees for me tonight.
iii   /pliyz downt weyt əndər ðə triyz fər miy tənayt/

4 I saw seashells on the seashore.

iv /ay sɔ siyšelz ɔn ðə siyšɔr/

5 Sticks and stones
   May break my bones
   But calling names
   Won't hurt me.

v /stiks ən stownz
   mey breyk may bownz
   bət kɔliŋ neymz
   wownt hərt miy/

An examination of the sentences above confirms the well-known
fact that the English alphabet is not completely phonemic, as the
term phonemic has been described above. One reason why it is not
phonemic is that the alphabetic system of modern English was
devised for the language before the period of modern English, and
between the time the system was devised and today the English
language has undergone many important sound changes, particularly in its vowel system as a result of the Great Vowel Shift. But
more importantly, the original spelling system was probably never
designed to be a phonemic one. Phonemic theory in the sense just
outlined is a very recent formalization, although undoubtedly certain
aspects of what was to become a phonemic theory were grasped
intuitively by many people before they were formalized by linguists.
Certainly alphabetic writing itself must have resulted from either
intuitive notions about the phonological structure of utterances or
the discovery of suitable techniques for determining such a phonological structure.

Most linguists who have tried to show the relevance of linguistic
findings to the teaching of reading have concentrated on the phonemic-graphemic correspondence problem. They have emphasized
that English spelling is best regarded as a symbolization of English
sounds and that it makes more sense to talk about how sounds are
represented by symbols in the writing system than to say how letters
are pronounced, because the latter approach is sure to create end-
less confusion, particularly for anyone unskilled in phonetics or
linguistics. They have urged that methods of teaching reading be
based on adequate analyses of the English sound system, on precise,
accurate statements of sound-symbol correspondences, and on cer-

tain psychological principles, such as training in the conscious discrimination of sound contrasts and presentation of regular patterns before irregular ones, for methods based on either misinformation about English or misunderstanding of language in general are less likely to succeed. Most linguists who have written about the teaching of reading have advocated the introduction of regular sound-symbol correspondences before less regular ones and strict control over the introduction of sight words, pointing out that the English spelling system will appear much more consistent to the beginning reader if the teacher approaches the problem of helping students to master it in this way. Their influence on the teaching of reading, particularly on that branch of reading instruction known as phonics, has been all to the good when it has been felt. For too long phonics has been linguistically unsound and has needed a good basis in defensible linguistic and phonetic information. Most linguistic reading programs have in reality turned out to be little more than phonics programs with a new type of phonics instead of an older, rather unscientific phonics.

Linguists have also stressed the fact that English punctuation devices are related to intonation patterns and that the good reader must recognize and react to these subtle graphic devices, which indicate the pauses, stresses, and pitches of the spoken equivalents of the written sentences. In acquiring this ability the reader has to relate syntactic, lexical, and phonological information. Pause, stress, and pitch phenomena have always created difficulties of description for linguists, because they are not easily handled by most linguistic procedures. Usually described as *suprasegmental phonemes*, they are related to such lexical and grammatical units as words, compounds, phrases, and sentences. Some linguists have actually used them to define these other units. Because of the way that pause, pitch, and stress phenomena combine into intonation patterns and the way these patterns coincide with grammatical patterns, it has even been claimed that a proper reading of a sentence requires a covert reading that echoes its overt pronunciation, so that all vowel reductions, pitch levels, stress patterns, pitch terminals, and so on of a spoken sentence may be somehow created or recreated in the "reading."

The insistence on phoneme-grapheme correspondences has not been without its difficulties. For example, there are the difficulties of vowel reduction and consonant deletion. In English many unstressed vowels reduce to schwa [ə] and many unstressed syllables show consonant deletion, so that *I can go* becomes /ay kən gow/, *I should have* becomes /ay šudəv/, and *I am going to go* becomes /aym gənə gow/, all of which are perfectly good English pronunciations and may be observed quite regularly in ordinary spoken usage. This vowel and consonant reduction creates problems in deciding exactly which kind of utterances should be used for phoneme-grapheme correspondence counts: those of extremely careful, precise, even "over-enunciated" speech or those of relaxed everyday usage.

It is not surprising that attempts have been made periodically to reform English spelling by applying some variety of the phonemic principle in order to make the English spelling system more phonemic. These attempts have varied from minor tinkering with the existing orthography (by mixing upper and lower case letters, for example) to the devising of completely new orthographic symbols. The more radical the proposed changes, the more impossible seems the task of persuading the public to adopt the reform. Minor changes are, however, sometimes acceptable. The Initial Teaching Alphabet, with its well-thought-out orthographic alterations, its phonemic basis, and its deliberately limited goal of helping children to begin to read through the elimination of most spelling irregularities, is one of the more successful attempts to reform English spelling for a specific purpose. The proponents of *i.t.a.* claim that it is very successful in achieving this goal; although the evidence is still inconclusive, there may well be justification for their claim. However, alphabetic systems were probably never intended to represent phonological contrasts alone, ignoring information from the semantic and syntactic parts of language. Although most modern linguists decided to ignore such information in formalizing their phonemic theories, there is no reason to suppose that those people who actually devised the English orthographic system were similarly motivated. Certainly they seemed to take into account the fact that the alphabet was to be used by people who already spoke the language. Consequently it did not have to have an exclusively phonetic basis; it could also make use of the semantic and syntactic information which those who used it would have in addition to the phonological information at their disposal.

Today the kind of phonemic theory that excludes the use of lexical and grammatical information is under heavy attack, and many linguists no longer subscribe to the procedures for phonemicization in developing new writing systems discussed in the earlier part of this chapter. Instead these linguists maintain that a writing system should represent the morphophonemic contrasts in a language rather than the phonemic ones. They point out that readers have lexical and grammatical information at their disposal when they read, because they "know" the language, and therefore need only a simple set of instructions for using that knowledge. Approaching English orthography from such a perspective, these linguists can show that the lack of distinction in the English spelling system for the plural marking in *cats* and *dogs,* the s for both, is in actual fact a good representation for English, since the voicing difference [s]-[z] is entirely predictable. An English speaker cannot do anything else but pronounce the s that marks the plural as [s] after [t] and [z] after [g]; therefore, this [s]-[z] difference need not be symbolized in an efficient writing system, because it is completely predictable once the t and g are recognized. That *sip* and *zip* do have an [s]-[z] contrast is quite irrelevant. In the case of *sip* and *zip* the [s]-[z] difference is important and must be symbolized, because it is quite unpredictable in the sense that a speaker of English has a genuine choice between the two sounds in this environment. The two cases are quite different and the symbolization problems are also quite different. This approach to the English spelling system makes it appear to be a much better principled system than an approach that ignores the information other than phonological that readers bring to the reading task.

The morphophonemic basis of English spelling can be demonstrated most easily by reference to the formation of the plural marking of nouns and the third person and past markings of verbs. In the English spelling system most nouns are given a final s as a plural marker, and most verbs are given a final s as a third person singular marker and a final ed as a past tense marker. The result is that in English we write *two bats, two logs,* and *two judges; he fights, he sighs,* and *he snatches;* and *he baked, he begged,* and *he wounded.* (The d instead of ed in *baked,* the es instead of s in *snatches,* and the doubling of the g in *begged* are of no concern at the moment.) These inflections are the regular productive English inflections for plural, third person singular and past tense, the ones that are attached to new words in the appropriate word classes and to the majority of existing words in those classes. Irregular inflections such as *mice, criteria, has, was,* and *drank* may also be ignored for the moment, since they are special cases and in closed sets. In the English writing system both the plural of nouns and the third person singular of verbs are marked by *s,* but the two morphemes have three different phonetic realizations or allomorphs: [s], [z], and [əz]. Similarly, the past tense marking of verbs has three different phonetic realizations: [t], [d], and [əd]. In each case the particular phonetic realization required by the context is fully predictable; *bats* is read as *bat* + plural, *logs* as *log* + plural, and *judges* as *judge* + plural. There is no need to show the different phonetic realizations of the plurals with different symbols, because the correct phonetic values will be assigned automatically by any reader who speaks English, through phonological rules that he has no choice but to apply. Hence the *s* spelling for each of the phonetic variants of the plural is justified. The same reasons apply in the case of the *s* for third person singular and rather similar reasons for the *ed* spelling for the past tense in verbs. In each case the spelling captures an important rule that every native speaker knows intuitively. He knows that the endings of *bats, logs,* and *judges* represent the same meaning, and he is hardly aware that they are phonetically different. Certainly *bats* and *logs* seem to him to end much the same way, and the difference is not nearly as obvious as the difference he perceives between the initial sounds of *sip* and *zip.* The lack of a spelling difference in *bats* and *logs* and the presence of one in *sip* and *zip* is a good illustration that English orthography has a morphophonemic basis rather than a phonemic one.

Other less obvious justifications for existing English spellings may be seen in such words as *long, sing,* and *finger.* It might be objected that there should be no final *g* on *long* and *sing,* because they are pronounced as [lɔŋ] and [sɪŋ]. However, *long* like *strong* has a comparative form, and this form has a [g] in it: *longer* ([lɔŋgər]). The case for the *g* in *sing,* like that in *swing,* is different, because *singer* does not rhyme with *finger* in most dialects of English. The final *g* here has to be represented in the spelling to provide for a contrast between *sin* and *sing* ([sin] and [sɪŋ]) and also to distinguish an agent *-er* from a comparative *-er* in the derivational system of English. *Long* [lɔŋ] plus *-er* comparative becomes [lɔŋgər], just as **strong** becomes **stronger** with a [g]; however, **sing** [sɪŋ] plus *-er* agent becomes [sɪŋər], just as *ring* becomes *ringer* and *hang* becomes **hanger**. *Sin* becomes *sinner* [smər] with the same *-er* agent. **Finger** [fɪŋgər] is a different case again, because in *finger* there is no morpheme break in the middle of the word, and when there is no such break orthographic *-ng-* represents [ŋg]. One can easily understand how the existing spelling system captures important generalizations about English if he acknowledges that speakers (and therefore readers) of English know that the two *-er*'s are different, that *long* and *sing* are different parts of speech, one an adjective and the other a verb, and that *finger* like *anger* cannot be decomposed into separate units of meaning. He will also understand that certain phonological matters follow automatically from such generalizations—for example, a nasal symbolized as *n* before a *g* must be homorganic with the *g* (made in the same position) and must be [ŋ], and in certain circumstances the *g* may not be pronounced.

Some examples of English orthography have a spelling relationship not shown in the surface phonology. In the pairs *able/ability* and *nation/nationality,* for example, the vowel alternations in the first syllable in each pair are automatically produced by native speakers as soon as they recognize the underlying derivational patterns. A correct "sounding out" of *national* requires the reader to break *national* down into two units, *nation* and *-al,* and then to pronounce these two units together. He will automatically change the vowel in the first syllable from [e] to [æ].

Several attempts have been made in recent years to show the morphophonemic basis of English orthography (for example, Venezky, 1967), and to point out the underlying phonological system of English (for example, Hill, 1968, and Chomsky and Halle, 1968). Several very interesting points about English emerge from such studies, and these may provide some systematic basis for phonics instruction. Venezky, for example, discusses the problem of some of the orthographic conventions of English. English orthography uses such single letters as *x* and *q* and combinations like *th, ch,* and *dg* in special ways that have to be learned by beginning readers, as in *ax, quick, thin, church,* and *judge. W* and *y* also have their peculiarities of use, because they can be used to represent either vowel values or consonant values. For example, *y* represents a vowel in *sky, by,* and *analysis* and a consonant in *young, you,* and *yes.* The two symbols *u* and *i* alternate with the symbols *w* and *y* respectively in certain spelling patterns. *U* and *w* alternate in pairs like *loud/ allow, taught/law,* and *quick/twin,* and *i* and *y* in *rejoice/joy* and *laid/lay.* The *o* in words such as *love, son,* and *won;* alternations such as the *c/k* alternation in *cat* and *kitten;* the *ca-/ci-* alternation in *cat* and *city;* and the *notice, noticing, noticeable* spelling differences must all be learned as spelling conventions.

All of these differences are of a different order from the next group, in which the five vowel symbols are used in certain systematic ways to show what have traditionally been called short and long, or checked and free, vowel differences, as shown in Table II.

Table II   Vowel Symbols in Checked and Free Patterns

Ortho-graphic Symbols	Short or Checked Vowel	Phonetic Value	Long or Free Vowel	Phonetic Value
a	apt fat hatter	[æ]	ape fate hater	[e]
e	hemp met better	[ɛ]	theme mete	[i]
i	imp sit dinner	[ɪ]	ice site diner	[ai]
o	opt rob comma	[ɔ]	pope robe coma	[o]
u	gulp run supper	[ʌ]	dupe rune super	[u]

However, the pairs of checked and free vowels show a further interesting correspondence, as illustrated in Table III, where each of the free vowels is shown to have a checked equivalent in a derived form.

Table III Vowel Symbols in Derivational Patterns

Orthographic Symbol	Free Form	Checked Form
a	nation	national
	sane	sanity
	fable	fabulous
	angel	angelic
	(vain)	(vanity)
e	penal	penalty
	supreme	supremacy
	meter	metrical
	recede	recession
	(please)	(pleasant)
i	prime	primitive
	crime	criminal
	mime	mimic
	ignite	ignition
	divide	division
	design	designate
	sublime	sublimate
o	tone	tonic
	cone	conic
	repose	repository
	verbose	verbosity
	holy	holiday
u	reduce	reduction
	induce	induction

The existence of pairs of words like those in Table III suggests that the English spelling system preserves the relationship between a morpheme and its derivatives by using the same orthographic symbols for the vowel symbols in both. The shared orthographic symbol maintains the visual bond between the root morpheme and its derivative. It also preserves the underlying phonological relationship known to linguists as tense–lax that is almost certainly the basis of the long-short vowel distinction made by teachers of reading, and it gives a reader the information he needs to pronounce the derived form correctly.

There are similar interesting patterns of correspondence in other parts of the spelling system of English. For example, there is the consonantal patterning exemplified by such words as *bomb–bombastic, damn–damnable, sign–signal,* and *autumn–autumnal,* where the *b, n, g,* and *n* respectively of the base forms is unpronounced but becomes pronounced in the derived forms. The *b* in *bomb–bombastic* behaves quite differently from the *b* in *lamb, thumb,* and *debt,* where it is never pronounced. There are also patterns like *race–racial,* where the *ci* spelling in the derivative indicates the fact that the *c* is palatalized; *electric–electricity–electrician,* where the *c* indicates respectively the "hard" [k] (before pause), the "soft" [s] (before *-ity*), and the palatalized [š] (before *-ian*) variants of the basic final consonantal element in the word; and *permit–permissive-permission,* where a somewhat similar kind of alternation [t ~ s ~ š] is indicated in the orthography. In the spellings of such pairs and triplets as *médicine–medícinal, nátion–nátional–nationálity, pérson-pérsonal–personálity,* and *régular–regulárity* there is a preservation of the underlying basic shapes of the morphemes even though there are changes in stress that result in changes in the pronunciation of certain vowels; however, since both the assignment of stress and the vowel reduction are made quite automatically by native speakers of English, they need not be represented in the orthography.

In *The Sound Pattern of English* Chomsky and Halle (1968) have put forward a description of English phonology that attempts to explain such vowel, consonantal, and stress relationships. Chomsky and Halle postulate an underlying phonological system for English, which they symbolize in an orthography that closely resembles the one used to spell Standard English. They also set forth a number of rules to account for the varying pronunciations given by native speakers to a set of underlying phonological units, called "systematic phonemes." These rules account for the different pronunciations of the *a* in *nation–national,* the *e* in *concede–concession,* the *i* in *wide–width,* the *o* in *cone–conic,* and the *u* in *deduce–deduction.* Chomsky and Halle point out that English orthography is closely related to the set of systematic phonemes they propose for English. They point out that the orthography is intended for readers who can understand sentences and who therefore do not have to be supplied with certain phonetic information in a truly economical orthography. These readers have available a set of phonological habits (or rules) which determine how they pronounce what they recognize; an economical orthography does not need to be concerned with these habits, since native speakers have no choice but to behave in certain ways in pronouncing words and structures they recognize. Chomsky and Halle point out that a non-native speaker of English would need to have these phonetic rules for pronunciation made explicit and would require an orthography that would allow him to pronounce without necessarily understanding. Such an orthography would be of the phonemic kind described by Bloomfield and Fries. Native speakers do not need such an orthography, and Chomsky and Halle claim that Standard English orthography is actually almost as good as anyone could desire for English.

Chomsky and Halle describe a model of the reading process for native speakers that assumes they "know" the language. It employs a phonological model constructed in the form of a set of rules. The model attempts to capture what it is that native speakers know about the phonology of the language. There are, however, some difficulties in applying their description to beginning reading.

First, no claim is made that the phonological rules are "psychologically real" or even that they are fully correct, since the whole book is presented as a report of "work in progress" and not as a definitive study. Chomsky and Halle offer no more than a tentative model of an ideal system, accounting for certain facts about English phonology that interest them in the way required by their overall view of what a language is and what a linguistic description must be like.

Second, much of Chomsky and Halle's description is valid only for a particular kind of person—a highly literate one. The crucial question for teachers of beginning reading is how much of such a rich system of phonology as that postulated in *The Sound Pattern of English* can be ascribed to a six-year-old. The answer is that probably a great deal can be ascribed, for certainly a six-year-old assigns stress correctly, reduces vowels automatically, and makes the majority of surface phonetic contrasts without difficulty. Therefore a six-year-old undoubtedly possesses much of the basic phonological competence he will ever have. At the same time, it is likely that both the set of underlying phonological forms and the set of transformational rules that he uses to convert underlying phonological forms into sounds are more limited than the sets discussed in *The Sound Pattern of English*.

Third, the system put forward in *The Sound Pattern of English* appears to encode meaning into sound, in spite of the claims to neutrality between speaker and hearer that the authors have repeatedly made. Chomsky and Halle also point out how an awareness of surface structure is necessary if a speaker is to assign certain stress patterns correctly and make the rules operate properly in the production of sentences. The task that confronts a reader is to decode print to discover meaning, to get to meaning through print. The beginning reader must somehow give a syntactic reading to *American history teacher* as either a teacher of American history or an American who is a history teacher before he can pronounce the phrase correctly. The writing system does not mark surface structure, however, except in certain gross ways, such as by word spacing and punctuation marks. The beginning reader is therefore called upon to relate symbols to sounds at an age when his abilities may be quite different from those of sophisticated adults. Chomsky and Halle have commented as follows on this problem:

> There are many interesting questions that can be raised about the development of systems of underlying representation during the period of language acquisition. It is possible that this might be fairly slow. There is, for example, some evidence that children tend to hear much more phonetically than adults. There is no reason to jump to the conclusion that this is simply a matter of training and experience; it may very well have a maturational basis. Furthermore, much of the evidence relevant to the construction of the underlying

systems of representation may not be available in early stages of language acquisition. These are open questions, and it is pointless to speculate about them any further. They deserve careful empirical study, not only because of the fundamental importance of the question of "psychological reality" of linguistic constructs, but also for practical reasons; for example, with respect to the problem of the teaching of reading. (1968, p. 50)

This comment is a most interesting one because, if empirical evidence confirms Chomsky and Halle's suspicion, there would seem to be some justification for Bloomfield and Fries's approach. There would be justification for an approach which utilizes a taxonomic-phonemic, or broad phonetic, level of representation; which relates such a level to orthographic patterns; which excludes work with derivational patterning in favor of work with sound-letter associations; and which does not get involved with patterns of stress assignment in polysyllabic words, because one can assume a six-year-old already controls these patterns by virtue of the fact that he is a native speaker.

It could well be that the basic problem a child has in learning to read is in learning the association between a level of written symbols and a level of surface phonology, rather than between a level of written symbols and a level of deep phonology. For example, he must learn that *hatter:hater; petter:Peter; dinner:diner; comma: coma;* and *supper:super* show a systematic spelling difference associated with a systematic surface phonological difference. In the terminology used by reading teachers, he must learn that a double consonant indicates a short vowel and that a single consonant plus vowel indicates a long vowel. Even though the use of the letters *a, e, i, o,* and *u* in the above words is "correct" in Chomsky and Halle's terms, the child has the problem of cueing in to the visual task involved in decoding. Likewise, with a set of words like *metal, rebel, devil, Mongol,* and *cherub,* it is important that the child have available a strategy for approaching these words so that he can attempt to pronounce them as *metal* or *meetal, rebel* or *reeble,* and so on. It is of no help to him to be told that the spellings are the best ones for English because there are also English words like *metallic, rebellion, civilian, Mongolian,* and *cherubic.* A six-year-old is even less likely to know these derivatives than the base forms.

Any knowledge we may have about the best spellings for the second vowel in each word is more appropriate to teaching him to spell than to read—two very different tasks.

Basically what the child needs in beginning reading is a set of strategies for decoding print. No one really knows what strategies successful beginning readers do employ. It may well be that they do not use the strategies that teachers who believe in the various phonics approaches attempt to teach. These strategies, sometimes encoded into a set of statements called phonic generalizations, have been severely attacked by some linguists. However, a reading of *The Sound Pattern of English* makes some of them much more defensible than they were. Statements about final *e*'s making preceding vowels "long," about *i*'s before *gh* having their "long" sound, and about *c*'s being "soft" before *e*'s and *i*'s are very like certain statements found in Chomsky and Halle's book. It is extremely doubtful, though, that a child faced with a word like *ladder* or *lady* ever says to himself something like "*a* followed by a double consonant says [æ]" or "*a* followed by a single consonant and a vowel says [e]." It is far more likely that he tries to associate what he sees and what he can figure out about the *l*'s, the vowels, and the *d*'s with familiar words that might fit the context: *He climbed the ladder* or *He gave it to the lady*. In other words, he works with a set of probabilities and a set of rules he has internalized, using them to bring some kind of order to the task that confronts him. Reading is not just habitual recognition of known patterns; it involves the active application of principles and strategies and therefore is legitimately a type of thinking. Carroll (1964b) has written:

> . . . . at some point the child needs to see that there is a regularity in such pairs as *at-ate, fat-fate, hat-hate, mat-mate,* not by learning rules or verbalizing them, but by achieving consistent discriminative responses. At the same time he needs to learn that he must often adopt a somewhat experimental trial-and-error approach to the letter combinations in words like *come, dome, home, some.* He must also be taught to take account of context in such experimentation, or educated guessing. (p. 63)

It seems fair to say that during the initial stages of learning to read children must be taught:

1. To approach reading left to right, because there is a basic left-to-right ordering of orthographic, grammatical and lexical information in the surface structures of sentences (though this ordering is not in every case the most important one, for it is a characteristic of surface structures that they must be realized in time and space, whereas abstract deep structures have no such limitations)

2. To identify the discriminating attributes of letters (*b-d*) and of words (*mat-mate*), in order to guarantee control of the minimal recognition skills required in reading

3. To associate written symbols with spoken sounds on a basis which takes into account the fact that they already know all the sounds, most of the grammar, and a considerable part of lexicon of the language and they are being taught to make associations between what they know and what is on the page in front of them

4. To acquire a familiarity with the main patterns of inflection and derivation as these are represented in English spelling and as these are similar to and different from those found in writing; and

5. To make intelligent guesses at what any particular group of letters represents.

To be able to teach these skills teachers must have available to them an adequate theory of reading based on a defensible statement about the phonological structure of English, one that will offer more profound observations than do statements about surface phonetic details. They also need a statement about how that phonological structure is related to English orthography. Any reading pedagogy without these can hardly be adequate.

CHAPTER EIGHT

Dialect

Any language spoken over a large area and by a great number of people exhibits dialect differences. English, with its wide geographical distribution throughout the world and its several hundred million speakers, is spoken in widely divergent dialects. It is still one language, however, because the dialects are more or less mutually intelligible: the Highland Scot understands the Texan and the South Australian understands the West Indian with greater or lesser ease. Some of the dialects of English have more prestige than others: in England the dialect associated with a certain geographical area—the Southeast—and with certain social strata in that area—the middle and upper classes—generally has more prestige than, for example, the dialects of Yorkshire miners and Somerset farmers; in the United States the dialects of Boston and Charleston have traditionally had more prestige than those of New York or the Ozarks; and in Canada the dialect of Southern Ontario is regarded as more representative of Canadian speech than a Nova Scotian or Newfoundland dialect.

It is important to note that in each case the prestige of the dialect derives from a geographic, social, or political factor, or from a combination of these factors, rather than from any intrinsic characteristic of the dialect. The pronunciation [də] for the word *the* is no better or worse in any absolute sense than the pronunciation [ðə].

If the latter pronunciation is preferred by educated English speakers, it is because it is associated with speakers who typically hold preferred positions in society. Both pronunciations convey exactly the same amount of linguistic information, and neither is ever misunderstood. But [də] has connotations of lack of education and of social inferiority, whereas [ðə] is neutral in this regard. Therefore, [də] carries non-linguistic information which [ðə] does not: it is "marked" for social unacceptability. Even a small percentage of [də] pronunciations, as few as twenty percent, interspersed among [ðə] pronunciations will mark a speaker as a user of a nonstandard variety of speech. He might even be thought to use [də] consistently when he actually does not.

A child born of middle class parents in Kent, England, will learn to speak one variety of English and an inner-city child in New York City will learn to speak a very different one. Each variety, or dialect, will serve the needs of the child who speaks it and will allow him to function quite adequately within his environment. A linguist can find no reason for saying that one dialect is better than another. Each has its own system, its own contrasts, and its own resources, and they sound equally good to someone who has no knowledge of the language at all. The preference of some speakers for one dialect or the other is in fact a preference for the non-linguistic correlates of the dialect rather than for the dialect itself. It is a preference for certain non-linguistic things associated with either middle class Englishmen or inner-city New Yorkers rather than a linguistic preference.

In order to understand just what is involved in dialect differences and how these differences relate to the teaching of reading, it is necessary to understand how a language varies. One of the basic facts that has come out of linguistic research during the last century is that every language changes in time and changes differently in different places. The English of today is different from Shakespeare's English and both are different from the English of Chaucer, and so on, back through Alfred to the Anglo-Saxon conquest of England, and even beyond that point in time. And at each point in time, there have been dialect differences. Throughout the English speaking world today, the British, American, Canadian, Australian, and South African varieties of English differ from each other, and within each of these varieties there are dialects.

The American dialects differ in the same ways that other dialects do, principally in geographic distribution. Some speakers of American English pronounce *fog* and *hog* as [fɔg] and [hɔg], whereas others say [fag] and [hag]. Some speakers pronounce **Don** the same as *dawn* and *cot* the same as *caught,* whereas others make a distinction within each pair. In some areas words like *car, part,* and *butter* are given *r*-less pronunciations, but in other areas the *r*'s are pronounced. *Mary, merry,* and *marry* may be pronounced identically by one speaker, with a single vowel contrast by another, and with two vowel contrasts by still another. *Where* and *wear* may or may not be homophonous, just as *horse* and *hoarse* may or may not be. Using such distinctions as these, linguists can describe certain major dialect areas of the United States. There is a Northern area which is *r*-pronouncing and in which *tin* and *ten* are distinguished, *cow* is pronounced as [kau], *on* as [an], *greasy* as [grisɪ], *news* as [nuz], and *which* as [hwɪč]; there is a Midland area which is *r*-pronouncing and has the *tin–ten* distinction, [kæu] for *cow,* [ɔn] for *on,* [grizɪ] for *greasy,* [nuz] for *news,* and [wɪč] for *which;* and there is a Southern area which is *r*-less, which has no *tin–ten* distinction, and which has [kæu] for *cow,* [ɔn] for *on,* [grizɪ] for *greasy,* [nɪuz] for *news,* and [wɪč] for *which.* In addition to such phonological distinctions, there are grammatical and lexical ones, such as the Southern distinction between *you* and *you all* or the Northerner's *skunk* contrasting with the Southerner's *polecat.*

There are also differences within each dialect associated with age groupings, sex differences, ethnic origins, educational levels, occupations, and socio-economic statuses. Teenagers talk differently from adults, boys differently from girls, Americans of recent Polish origin differently from Americans of recent Mexican origin, college graduates differently from grade-school graduates, doctors differently from soldiers, and the very wealthy differently from the very poor. Since all these factors are important, dialect study is not easy to conduct, nor are the findings easy to interpret. The various dialect studies in the United States clearly demonstrate the difficulties of both data collection and data interpretation, whether they are the regional studies of the various atlas projects, or the sociolinguistic studies conducted in various large cities, or studies of children's speech, teenage speech, or trade speech. Shuy's very concise *Discovering American Dialects* (1967) provides one of the best short introductions to the topic of regional dialects, but unfortunately there are no equally good short introductions to the other topics mentioned.

Nonstandard dialects are even more difficult to describe than standard ones because of the social and political dimensions involved in any attempt to make satisfactory descriptions. The term *nonstandard* is preferred to *substandard,* because such dialects are different from standard dialects rather than inferior to them. They are neither primitive nor debased variations of a cultivated or educated standard language. Rather they are fully functional varieties of the language spoken by groups who have little or no social prestige. Nonstandard dialects have not been thoroughly studied, in some cases because they were felt to be inferior and hardly worthy of study and in other cases because of a desire to avoid a politically or socially sensitive problem, particularly when the dialect in question could be related to a distinct minority group. Although this sensitivity still exists in many places, linguists such as Labov, McDavid, and Shuy (see Shuy, 1965) have refused to let it deter them from scientific investigation, for they believe that many political, social, and educational problems cannot properly be solved if linguistic evidence is deliberately concealed or if solutions to the problems are based on anecdotal evidence rather than on systematic research.

Teachers of reading must recognize that dialect differences are to be expected within a language and that dialects are intrinsically equal. A so-called standard variety of English is but one dialect of English: the standard itself actually varies considerably from region to region within the English-speaking world. Dialect variation, either among various standard dialects or between the standard and nonstandard dialects within a region, is likely to be more evident to teachers in large urban areas than in rural areas because of population density, population migrations from rural areas, and concomitant rapid social change. The differences are much less noticeable in rural areas, where the population is more likely to be more homogeneous and stable and where the teachers are more likely to be of local origin. Like the children they teach, teachers move from rural areas into cities, not vice versa.

Children learn to read at an age when they are less conscious of dialect differences than their teachers. At this age, too, the linguistic influence of their peers is much more important than the exhortations of adults, a fact to which anyone with young children in school can testify. There is reason to believe that children do not understand what a teacher is trying to do when she attempts to change some linguistic habit they have. Children can change their linguistic habits and modify their dialects with ease, but they apparently cannot do so consciously; rather, according to some evidence, much of the modification is the result of unconscious assimilations that occur within peer groups, so that a child's language tends to reflect that of his associates rather than that of his parents when these two varieties are markedly different. In this process of language change the factor known as age grading is therefore extremely important. For example, Dillard has claimed to have found evidence that certain five- and six-year-olds in Washington, D.C., say sentences like *He is a nice little girl* in which there is no *he-she* differentiation, but that such forms are not found at later age levels. Similarly, *he brother* for *his brother* and *she book* for *her book* disappear in the same social group between the ages of nine and fourteen. It appears, then, that preference for certain linguistic forms is related to certain age levels and that children in a sense "naturally" use the forms in their dialect characteristic of their age level. They also apparently find it difficult to change these forms as a result of external pressure; the changes that do occur seem to come from within the speaker subconsciously rather than as a result of conscious attempts to "correct" speech or to apply rules given by adults. Teachers tend to stress the importance of corrections to young children; in fact such corrections may be of little importance.

On the other hand, adolescents do seem to be able to accept corrections of some kinds and to modify their linguistic behavior accordingly, but such attempts at self-correction during adolescence create their own problems. The linguistic habits of adolescents are very strong, as witnessed by the fact that they have much more difficulty in learning a foreign language than do elementary-school children. Deliberate attempts by teachers or even by adolescents themselves to change dialects can lead to the partial destruction of longstanding habits and to only a partial mastery of the new habits which are meant to replace the old ones. Sometimes the consequence is a kind of linguistic schizophrenia, because the hybrid dialect that results may be neither one thing nor another, acceptable neither to speakers of the nonstandard or regional dialect nor to speakers of the standard dialect. In such a case, the speaker has in effect cut himself off from both groups and become a linguistic misfit. Of course, most people do not become misfits to this extent, but most of us know a few speakers who exhibit some dialect mixture or uncertainty about usage. Again, this situation is not typical of English alone. Bloomfield (1927), for example, gives some very interesting examples of similar phenomena among speakers of Menomini.

Many teachers tend to suffer on occasion from the pains of linguistic uncertainty, because of their social antecedents, their aspirations, and the roles they are forced to play in society. The result is sometimes a dogmatic position on matters of usage but an actual usage that varies considerably from that prescribed by the dogma, to the bewilderment of the students. The adoption of both a dogmatic position and language use consistent with that position, on the other hand, is apt to lead to student hostility towards a dialect never heard anywhere outside the classroom. Linguistic habits are strong; they should not be tampered with lightly and with little regard for the consequences.

The dialect represented in books such as textbooks and other expository prose bears more resemblance to certain spoken dialects than to others. The kind of language that is placed in the mouths of characters in novels and stories, on the other hand, may be of two kinds: language that makes no claim to represent the actual speech of the characters, particularly its phonetic flavor, and language that attempts to do just that. The second type results in two kinds of dialect writing. One kind, called "eye dialect," reports the words of speakers in such spellings as *wuz* for *was,* or *I could of* for *I could've* or *I could have,* or *I'm gonna* for *I'm going to.* Each of these written expressions is perfectly normal spoken English, but some authors use the spellings indicated only for certain social types in their books, reporting the speech of a villain or an underworld type in forms like *wuz* and *gonna* and that of protagonists with *was* and *going to.* Such a variety of dialect writing as this is hardly more than a trivial literary device of little artistic consequence. The second kind of dialect writing is very different, because it actually informs the reader of the differences between the speech of a character in a story and that of the reader: the author uses such spellings as *nufin' (nothing), skyool (school), larnt (learned), 'cos (because), wi'* *(with),* and so on. By using such spellings, a skilled author may convey a very accurate impression of the speech of his characters, whereas eye dialect tells a reader nothing about how the speech differs, or might differ, from standard English. The language of expository prose is a dialect of a different kind. It is fixed by spelling and word writing conventions and very deliberately mirrors the linguistic usages of a standard language (rather than those of non-standard speech or distinct regional varieties), particularly in its lexical selections and grammatical devices.

Differences between standard written forms and nonstandard dialect forms may create obstacles if they are not clearly understood by teachers. For example, the student who habitually says **They was going** may be faced with the task of making a response in oral reading to a printed **They were going.** As Goodman (1964) has argued, if the teacher is concerned that the student understand what the writer intended, she may expect the student to read **They were going** as **They was going.** She should consider this response to be perfectly adequate, because the student's **They was going** and the writer's **They were going** mean the same thing in that they are linguistically equivalent in the two dialects. The teacher may be tempted to tell the student that the words are actually **They, were,** and **going,** and to insist that he read the phrase as **They were going** and not as **They was going.** But it is doubtful that such information will be useful to the student in his task and, as Goodman shows, on occasion it may not even register. The student who reads **were** as **was** in such circumstances is actually reading very well in the sense of reading for meaning, for he is showing that he has understood what was written by reproducing it orally *in his own dialect.* Similarly, linguists visiting classrooms have heard children who say **fine** where the standard dialect requires **find** read the latter aloud as **fine,** only to be told that they have misread what is in front of them. Again such children are reading well, so well that they feel comfortable enough to "translate" the visual symbols into the phonology of the dialect that has meaning for them. There is no reason to demand that such children say **find** in oral reading, since the requirement that they learn a new phonological rule about the pronunciation of final consonants could well impose an obstacle to comprehension.

When teachers are confronted with the task of teaching reading to children who speak a nonstandard dialect, they should be aware that the task of modifying a nonstandard dialect is a task of a different kind from that of teaching reading, and the two tasks should be kept strictly apart at all times. To attempt both tasks together is probably to do both badly. Teachers must recognize that children who speak a nonstandard dialect control a complete phonological system that they can learn to relate to the English spelling system. This relationship may not be the same as that which holds for a standard dialect, but the differences are relatively minor ones: certain phonemic contrasts may be different in a small number of environments and the actual sounds used to realize the phonemic contrasts may differ. The words *beat, bit, bait, bet, bat,* and *bite* are almost certain to contrast just as they do in a standard dialect, but *pin* and *pen* may not contrast. This lack of contrast of /i/ and /e/ before /n/ will be quite systematic, however; it is not unlike the lack of contrast usually found in vowels before /r/ in such words as *bird, word,* and *curd.* The precise phonetic values of the vowels in *bait* and *bite* might differ from those used by the teachers, but they will be used no less consistently, so that *bite, night,* and *height* will rhyme in the nonstandard dialect. The teacher's task is to relate the entire phonological system controlled by the children to the English writing system, so that they can understand that English employs an alphabetic writing system which they must master in order to be able to read.

Even in those cases where the phonological rules of the dialect produce homophonous pairs, like *paw* and *Paul,* or homophonous triplets, like *go, goal,* and *gold* (Labov, 1967), teachers should allow for the systematic nature of these phenomena. The problem of homophony in standard dialects is generally well understood by teachers, who are aware of such pairs as *meet* and *meat, rite* and *right,* and *way* and *weigh.* The spellings of these words are to some extent systematic, and children do have principles for guidance in learning to read them. The *paw, Paul* and *go, goal, gold* patterns are also systematic. If these words are homophonous in a nonstandard dialect, so will other pairs and triplets be homophonous. The pairs and triplets will also exhibit a strong spelling resemblance: *bow, bowl, bold; dough, dole, doled; foe, foal, fold; hoe, hole, holed* or *hold; Poe, poll* or *pole, polled; row, roll, rolled; sow, soul* or *sole, sold;* and *toe, toll, told.* Teachers of reading should build on the fact that the sounds of nonstandard dialects are systematic, that English orthography is for the most part systematic, and that the two systems are related. There is no need to teach children a new dialect to teach them to read. Such teaching will almost certainly lead to dialect-mixing and consequently an undermining of the very systems and relationships that are utilized in every method of teaching reading, whether overtly as in phonics methods or covertly as in whole-word methods. Methods that succeed with speakers of standard dialects can succeed with speakers of nonstandard dialects, provided that teachers realize they are teaching reading, not speaking; they should deliberately exploit the patterns of the nonstandard dialects, as Fries did for standard dialects.

Grammatical differences among dialects may be more difficult to overcome than the phonological ones we have mentioned. These differences are also more conspicuous in a society in which "bad" grammatical usage is considered to be more reprehensible than the pronunciation of grammatically correct utterances in a regional accent. The grammatical variations in a dialect may be quite different from standard usages, such as *I seen him, You all are going,* and *I ain't got none.* Sometimes a dialect may have no overt difference where standard English has; for example, nonstandard *He kneel down* might be equivalent to both *He kneels down* and *He kneeled down* in standard usage. *Kneel* may be the phonological realization of both *kneels* and *kneeled* because a phonological rule operates to simplify final consonant clusters, so that both final //lz// and //ld// become [1]. The same rule may operate to make *cold* homophonous to *coal* and *find* homophonous to *fine.* The speaker who reads *kneels* and *kneeled* as *kneel* may very well distinguish *drink* and *drunk* (or *drank*) and have two pronunciations of *read,* one rhyming with *reed* in *I now read well* and the other with *red* in *Yesterday I read well.* In other words, he has a tense distinction between past and non-past in his verbal system, but in certain cases the distinction is neutralized by a phonological rule peculiar to the dialect in question.

The different rules for various dialects can have very interesting consequences. Stewart (1967) has discussed a nonstandard dialect in which there appears to be a contrast between *He busy* and *He be busy.* *He busy* is equivalent to "He is busy (at the moment)" and *He be busy* to "He is busy (always)," just as *He workin'* is equivalent to "He's working right now" and *He be workin'* to "He's working (steadily)." In this case there is an important difference in what linguists refer to as *aspect* in the verb system. A student who speaks such a dialect, confronted with the task of reading a sentence like *He is busy at school,* may have a problem in getting the meaning, since standard English lacks the aspect distinction possessed by his dialect. The student must internalize (or process) the sentence as referring to "at the moment" or "always" and therefore force a distinction that the text does not have. If he reads the sentence as *He busy at school,* he has chosen the former and as *He be busy at school* he has chosen the latter. If the teacher insists that the student read the sentence as *He-is-busy-at-school,* the student may not be able to arrive at any interpretation and may actually end up doing little more than barking at print. The widespread notion that non-standard dialects are poverty-stricken in their linguistic resources is indefensible; the above example is but one instance where the falsity of this belief may be readily demonstrated.

The preceding discussion may lead one to conclude that there is little need, as Goodman (1965) has indicated, for speakers of non-standard dialects to learn to read through the use of special materials, different from traditional materials in either spelling system or grammatical patterns. There may be a case for materials with different cultural content and different vocabulary from traditional materials, but this is not a point for linguists or even anthropologists and sociologists to settle by themselves; it bears directly on the philosophy and purpose of education, and in such matters linguists, anthropologists, and sociologists are but interest groups like any others. Any such person who says that the books used to teach children who live in rural Mississippi or in a New York ghetto should reflect on the one hand the life of that rural area and on the other the life of that ghetto is actually stepping beyond his competence.

It has been claimed that speakers of certain nonstandard dialects have acquired certain cognitive restrictions not experienced by speakers of standard dialects. This point of view is not, of course, a new one. The Sapir-Whorf hypothesis states that speakers of different languages tend to view the world differently as a result of speaking these different languages, and there is no reason to suppose that, if the hypothesis is correct for different languages, it should not also be correct for different dialects within a language.

In addition, one could hypothesize that the cognitive differences within a language would be far more subtle than those between unrelated languages. However, it should be pointed out that the evidence in support of the Sapir-Whorf hypothesis is far from conclusive.

Many psychologists have looked at the same problem of the relationship of language and cognition and have devised their own hypotheses about the relationship. Bernstein (1964, 1967), for example, has hypothesized that speakers of different social dialects have access to different codes. He is more concerned with social than regional dialects and claims that social dialects may be distinguished from each other in terms of what they allow their speakers to do—that is, what kind of messages they allow. According to Bernstein, middle- and upper-class dialects are elaborated codes that allow their speakers to say novel things, to think abstract thoughts, and to take part in freewheeling discussion. The lower-class dialects on the other hand, are restricted codes that confine their users to impersonal, disjunctive, and concrete types of language. They make for highly predictable content, assume a shared interest of speaker and listener in the topic, and draw heavily on extra-linguistic cues such as facial expressions and gestures. Speakers of middle- and upper-class dialects have access to both elaborated and restricted codes, using the latter for "small talk" and various social rituals, but lower-class speakers have access only to the restricted variety. Like the Sapir-Whorf hypothesis, this hypothesis is intriguing rather than convincing, for much the same reason. Both hypotheses seem untestable, for each makes the claim that language controls social behavior rather than that social behavior controls language. In the absence of a procedure for isolating social behavior from linguistic behavior, it seems impossible to test the claims of either Sapir and Whorf or Bernstein. The claims have resulted in much discussion, but essentially this discussion has lacked scientific rigor.

Still other psychologists, principally Piaget (Berlyne, 1957) and Vygotsky (1962), have speculated on the development of cognitive processes in children and on the internalization of speech. Piaget has tried to relate the stages of development through which children go on their way to maturity to the development of both language and thought. He has postulated five distinct stages of development: a sensori-motor stage, from birth to two years; a stage of preconceptual thought, from two to four years; a stage of intuitive thought, from four to seven years; a stage of concrete operations, from seven to eleven years; and finally a stage of formal operations, from eleven to fifteen years. As children progress through these stages they exhibit different types of behavior, some of which is reflected in the kind of language they use, such as the explanations they give for natural phenomena. Piaget's theory, based as it is on a small sample from which it is not easy to generalize, must be regarded as suggestive rather than proved. It has intrigued other developmental psychologists but, until recently, has had little influence on the thinking of psychologists who are interested in current linguistics. The latter psychologists are concerned with problems of an entirely different kind. Vygotsky's interest has been in showing how children gradually learn to "internalize" speech so that the overt words of child speech become the covert thoughts of the adult. Again his influence has not been great on linguistically oriented psychologists. There seems little reason to believe that the kinds of psychological processes that have fascinated both Piaget and Vygotsky are of great importance in considering children's dialect differences, whether regional or social in origin. If children do go through developmental stages or do "internalize" speech as they get older, there is no reason to assume that either development is correlated with one particular variety of a language rather than another.

Recent work in generative-transformational grammar by Chomsky and his associates has added new dimensions to the problem of dialect differentiation. Chomsky (1964) has suggested, for example, that dialects differ from each other in relatively minor ways and that language—that is, the abstract system that underlies the various dialects—is highly resistant to change in time. It is interesting to note that the underlying phonological system usually proposed for Modern English shows considerable resemblance to the system postulated for older stages of the language, particularly to Middle English. The rules that convert this underlying phonological system into phonetic representations are very similar to those that historical linguists have postulated to show the development of Middle English to Modern English. In this view, speakers of English over many generations have added, deleted, or reordered a rather small number of what may actually be called low-level phonetic rules. It is these phonetic rules that have changed rather than the underlying system itself. Dialects differ from each other not in the underlying system, which is actually the same for each dialect, but in some of the phonetic rules employed to realize utterances in that system, or even in the different ordering among dialects of what is really the same set of phonetic rules.

The validity of such a simple statement of the relationships among dialects has been questioned. If it is valid, it means that superficially quite disparate dialects of a language have a disparateness which can be characterized by a rather small number of special low-level phonetic rules and have almost identical deep structures, semantic structures, and underlying phonological systems. Like the previously mentioned hypotheses concerning language and cognition, this interesting statement will be very difficult to test empirically. It is an artifact of the generative-transformational model that deep structures may be the same among different languages and dialects. The rules that convert deep structures to phonetic realizations—that is, actual sentences—are those that the linguist finds necessary within the theoretical constraints he has imposed on himself, and, as Chomsky himself has pointed out (1965, p. 9), they are not to be considered psychological or performance rules. It is difficult to be certain about what consequences for teaching follow from such observations. One consequence could well be that English spelling—which has not substantially changed in hundreds of years and which is the same for all dialects and varieties of English—is satisfactory as a representation of just those phonological facts that need to be represented for any dialect of modern English. Individual variations in different dialects are idiosyncratic, predictable, and, therefore, to be ignored by teachers of reading.

Lenneberg's work (1967) on the biological basis of language is also intriguing from the point of view of both language acquisition and dialect acquisition. Lenneberg considers language to be a special kind of categorizing ability possessed by human beings. Other animals can categorize, too, because they react to their environments in systematic ways and acquire this ability in an orderly manner. When human beings use language they are categorizing, the main difference between this kind of categorizing and other kinds being one of the open-ness or infinite productivity of linguistic categorizing. This point of view is very like Chomsky's view that language activity is essentially a creative and novel activity. Like Chomsky,

Lenneberg regards the ability to learn a language as an innate ability possessed by the human organism, although he does not regard it as qualitatively different from other abilities. Lenneberg regards the environment as having considerable importance in the development of this innate ability, because at certain stages proper development requires that certain stimuli be present in the environment so that the organism can "resonate." The child is ready to do certain things at certain times, and it is doubtful that he can be "forced" like a hothouse plant, particularly in something like language development. Of course, the opposite is also true: in an environment without language, obviously the child cannot find the stimuli he needs, and an impoverished linguistic environment may provide stimuli of a very different kind from a rich linguistic environment.

The word *may* is deliberately chosen. What kind of stimuli and what types of linguistic experience a child requires to develop his full language ability are quite unknown. The child makes such a massive contribution to the language-learning task that apparently almost any linguistic environment would provide him with all the linguistic stimuli he requires to develop his full linguistic ability, even though an impoverished environment might limit the variety of uses he makes of language. The resonance theory does not conflict with the notion of social or regional dialect learning, because a child must obviously resonate to the language around him. There is also little reason to suppose that the differences that result from the differences in stimuli result in anything but minor differences in the child's linguistic competence. These differences may be of little or no linguistic consequence; however, the social consequences of performance differences may be considerable.

CHAPTER NINE

Reading: A New Perspective

Having looked at the teaching of reading from various points of view, all of them with a deliberate linguistic coloring, we may now attempt a definition of reading. When a person reads a text, he is attempting to discover the meaning of what he is reading by using the visual clues of spelling, his knowledge of probabilities of occurrence, his contextual-pragmatic knowledge, and his syntactic and semantic competence to give a meaningful interpretation to the text. Reading is not a passive process, in which a reader takes something out of the text without any effort or merely recognizes what is in the text. Nor does it appear to be a process in which he first recognizes what is on the page and then interprets it, a process in which a stage of decoding precedes a stage of involvement with meaning. There is little reason to suppose that there are two such discrete, non-overlapping stages. Reading is instead an active process, in which the reader must make an active contribution by drawing upon and using concurrently various abilities that he has acquired.

These abilities are of many different kinds. For example, there is the ability to associate certain sounds and certain letters. The reader must be able to react to significant rather than nonsignificant visual clues. He must also be able to use both short- and long-term memories effectively during the processing involved in reading. These abilities are not used automatically in all circumstances, because even the best readers make some mistakes; such mistakes indicate that the processing called for was incompletely or inaccurately carried out. The processing itself is not just processing of visual signals in order to convert these signals into some kind of covert speech. The conversion is not the end point of the process, because semantic and syntactic processing are necessary in addition to the processing of the visual signals.

Semantic and syntactic processing require a knowledge of the language—knowledge in the sense of competence—and they require this knowledge to be used actively. One cannot read a foreign language (except in the sense of barking at print) unless one has some underlying competence in that language, some training in its orthographic principles, and some knowledge of the subject matter, and can bring all these to bear on the task. A child cannot learn to read English unless he has some underlying competence in the English language (though this competence may be added to as a result of reading experiences). He must learn to react to the orthography, and ideally the subject-matter he is asked to read about should touch on something within his experience or be relevant to that experience in some way. Given these conditions, he will find the task of learning to be a meaningful one.

In beginning reading instruction considerable emphasis must be placed on teaching the association of orthography to phonology. This association is not as simple as certain claims have made it out to be, however, nor should it be the only area of concentration. Certain claims too about the relationships of symbols to sounds are open to question. For example, the claims about the importance of "silent" speech or about the mediational role of "internalized" speech, in understanding how people learn to associate symbols with sounds, demand serious consideration but are as yet unsubstantiated. Similarly, statements about what is regular and irregular in English orthography and how and why the irregularities must be controlled in beginning reading texts are sometimes conflicting. There is also conflicting opinion about the need to modify existing English orthography or to use only one type of print or to teach minimal letter and word shapes in contrast with each other, just as one might teach minimal phonological pairs. In the area of sentence types there is discussion about the desirability of restricting the content of readers to some of the simple recurring superficial patterns of the child's spoken language rather than including patterns that are infrequent or complex.

Linguists cannot provide complete answers to many of these problems because the problems are not exclusively linguistic. In every case there are variables other than linguistic ones to be considered. The problems are mainly pedagogical, and while linguists can provide some help in finding solutions, they cannot provide total solutions. There appears to be no more justification for talking about *a linguistic method* or various *linguistic methods* of teaching reading, particularly beginning reading, than for talking about a linguistic method or methods of teaching a foreign language. Linguistic methods are methods that linguists employ in doing linguistic research and possibly in teaching linguistics. Reading is not linguistics. It has a large linguistic content, but it also has content that is nonlinguistic; consequently, methods for teaching reading must draw on other sources in addition to linguistic ones. But such methods should build on sound linguistic knowledge.

It is also apparent that children will learn to read only by being given help with just that task, and that they do not learn to read by being told about the task. They do not learn to read by learning rules about what to do when they are confronted with certain difficulties, particularly when these rules are either too sophisticated, complicated, or inconsistent to be applied with a reasonable chance of success. They must learn to relate certain sounds to certain symbols, to distinguish *d* from *b* and *mat* from *mate,* to recognize that left to right direction is important as in *dog* vs. *god* and *top desk* vs. *desk top,* to recognize that the grammatical signals of written language are basically those of spoken language, and to use contextual clues in the decipherment of written texts, as in resolving the ambiguity of *He gave her a bow.* A few very basic rules such as those that apply to the *c* in *city* and *cat,* the *igh* in *fight,* and the *gh* in *enough* may be useful to beginning readers; however, it is doubtful that teaching children long lists of unordered phonic generalizations has any real benefit.

Of course, children do learn something which might be called a set of rules that they use in reading, because they do learn to read with greater or lesser success. Even the mistakes they make show them to be employing inappropriate rules rather than exhibiting randomized behavior. A child learns to read *city* and *cat* correctly as the result of experience with words beginning *ci-* and *ca-* and with his unconscious assimilation of the rule that almost always *c* followed by one group of vowel letters is associated with an [s] sound and by another group with a [k] sound. He may not be able to verbalize the rule, any more than he could tell you how he ties his shoe laces; but just as he can demonstrate that he knows the rules for tying shoe laces by tying shoe laces, so he can demonstrate his knowledge of the rules for pronouncing *c* by reading *city* and *cat* correctly. His knowledge of the rules is demonstrated by his performance and it is unnecessary for him to learn to verbalize a statement about what he has learned, that is, about what he knows. In studying the linguistic and reading performance of children, it would be well for a teacher to try to arrive at an understanding of what unconscious rules a particular child is applying to his tasks. It would also be wise to see the whole of the child's behavior as rule-governed, so that "mistakes" may be regarded as instances of applying inappropriate rules, rather than as the results of random behavior. In fact, the whole notion of "mistake" and "error" could well be discarded in favor of this kind of approach. Admittedly, not every mistake will be explicable in these terms, but it seems more fruitful to hypothesize that "mistakes result from the application of rules which are different from the rules of mature language users" than to hypothesize that "mistakes are instances of random (or perverse) behavior."

Reading requires certain perceptual skills that are not required for spoken language and, conversely, does not require certain perceptual skills required for spoken language. It has been claimed that when we read we "hear" what we read, that the visual symbol somehow triggers an aural one. While there is some evidence for silent speech (Edfeldt, 1960) and for the claim that speech perception has a motor basis, this evidence is by no means conclusive. It is well known that receptive control of language always exceeds productive control, that silent reading speed often exceeds aural comprehension speed, and that some people learn to read English who cannot or do not speak English for various reasons. While there is in every normal human being the capacity for language acquisition, this capacity can apparently be realized by linguistic stimuli other than aural stimuli, even though the latter are those to which most people actually do respond (or resonate). A normal child reacts naturally to the spoken language around him, and it provides him with all the stimuli he needs to become a speaker of the language. Some of those stimuli apparently come from within the child himself, from his innate propensities to learn a language. A child who is not normal, who is deaf or dumb or both, still has these propensities but must react to different external stimuli. His task may be much more difficult, but it is probably never impossible.

Reading is a different kind of linguistic performance from listening, just as listening is from speaking. The range of understanding in listening is greater than the range of production in speaking, and the range of understanding of written material is usually greater than that of spoken material. The latter is true mainly because one can read and reread, and thereby control the speed of the processing of the content that is being read. The material to be read is often rather different from that met in listening, however, and these differences can create difficulties. In general, written language is more deliberate, more complex, more heavily edited, and less redundant than spoken language, and it offers no opportunity to question the writer in order to seek clarification of his statements.

In both kinds of performance the individual makes a large personal contribution; as often as not, he hears what he wants to hear and reads what he wants to read rather than what was originally said or written. Comprehension is not a passive process. The comprehender must continually make hypotheses about what he is hearing or reading, attempt to match these hypotheses with other data he has available to him, and modify the hypotheses if they are inadequate.

Sometimes, of course, people adopt processing strategies that result in selective listening or reading, strategies that in effect allow them to ignore data that do not conform to their hypotheses. The result is a mishearing or misreading of the original content, a type of "mistake" that is a direct consequence of the contribution of the comprehender to the process of comprehension. For example, we sometimes anticipate words in a conversation or text only to discover ourselves to be wrong, or we do not wait for sentences to be completed because we assume we know what their endings will be, or we miss spelling mistakes because we are more concerned with meaning than with proofreading. Many of the mistakes students make in reading are made because the students have adopted inappropriate strategies in their processing. In the later stages of reading instruction, when reading for implications and reading between the lines become an important part of instruction, the possibilities for adopting inappropriate strategies increase. That errors and mistakes do occur in these circumstances should be expected; indeed it would be well to avoid the use of such terms as "errors" and "mistakes" in discussing such varieties of linguistic performance. As we have seen, these mistakes are generally perfectly explicable, because they are principled, motivated, and rule-governed.

One of the most interesting attempts to explain what happens when children make mistakes in reading has come from Goodman (1967). Goodman has shown that children reading unfamiliar textual material are forced to play what he calls a "psycholinguistic guessing game." The child must draw upon the rules he has internalized to read the novel text. He must try out the knowledge he has acquired of sound-symbol relationships, grammatical patterning, semantic collocations, and the real world in an attempt to impose some kind of order or meaning on the text. He must adopt a strategy that allows him to draw upon these different varieties of knowledge concurrently, and he must be prepared to make hypotheses, more or less educated guesses. Sometimes he will guess incorrectly, so that his responses will not conform to those of a mature reader, but his guesses will rarely be unmotivated; they will be "miscues," in Goodman's terms, rather than mistakes. The miscues can provide a great deal of insight into the particular strategies that the child is using, into the kind of psychological and linguistic—hence psycholinguistic—processes he is using subconsciously. Naturally, one can do no more than infer these processes from the responses, but it is still possible to give a fairly accurate account of the kind of reading competence that underlies the observed reading behavior. A reader's miscues in reading are evidence that his competence in reading varies from that of a mature reader, not that he lacks reading competence.

The competence that a reader uses is not the same competence that interests the linguist attempting to write a grammar for English. The two are not unrelated, however. Both are models of ideal systems. The linguist's model is the ideal system that characterizes the language; the reading researcher's model is the system that the reader has access to in his attempts to comprehend what he is reading. The latter model includes the linguistic competence of the reader that is relevant to his task. But it also includes nonlinguistic content, because the task is a perceptual and cognitive one, involving many competences other than that which interests the linguist. Both models must make allowance for performance characteristics, too: speakers and readers make mistakes, find their memories overburdened, and get confused as they react to inappropriate stimuli. Such phenomena, however, must be clearly distinguished from those that seem directly to manifest competence. People generally know when they have made a mistake, when they cannot remember how a sentence began, and when they are confused. It is important, therefore, that teachers distinguish this kind of knowledge from that kind which leads a reader to read *dog* as *bog* and *He's growing* as *He goin'*, in the belief that he has responded correctly.

One interesting set of performance variables is related to oral reading. There appear to be more performance variables in oral reading than in silent reading, because there is an extra set of production variables involved in the task. This extra set adds new complications to the already complicated task of studying where the process of comprehension may break down. In both silent and oral reading, the reader is required to get the meaning from the print in front of him. To find out whether or not the reader did get the meaning, one can use several methods. The reader can be asked to read the passage aloud, to answer questions, or to do something else—for example, to perform an action. In such ways one may attempt to discover if the process of comprehension has been completed. This process may break down in two critical places. The reader may or may not understand what was written and may or may not communicate that understanding or lack of understanding. He may understand and indicate that he understood; he may not understand and indicate that he did not understand; he may understand but fail to indicate this fact; and he may not understand but seem by his response to have understood. In judging a student's success in reading, we try to safeguard against the third and fourth possibilities, but we are not always successful. For this reason we must be cautious before we say that someone does not comprehend either what we say to him or what we require him to read.

The teaching of reading must be clearly distinguished from the teaching of speaking. Children come to school already speaking a dialect of the language, and it should be possible to teach them to read by drawing upon the language competence they exhibit in that dialect. There is an important distinction between students who have certain kinds of performance limitations, such as memory, perceptual, and motor limitations, and students who speak nonstandard dialects. Students of the first type have congenital or acquired deficiencies for which reading teachers must compensate. Students of the second type may or may not, of course, exhibit some of the same problems and as a group may actually have a greater incidence of such problems because of various deprivations in their background, but they should not be treated in the same way as the first group when they do not have these problems.

A student who says *wif* because he has a physical defect (and the loss of teeth should not be regarded as a physical defect in this sense) should be treated quite differently from one who says *wif* because that pronunciation of *with* is a feature of his dialect. To send both students to the speech therapist for the same "treatment" is a tragic mistake. The same may be true of pronunciations like *wed* for *red, Buce* for *Bruce,* and *fevver* for *feather.* To regard such pronunciations as obstacles in learning to read is extremely unwise. A teacher might be tempted to accept the pathological or maturational *wif* and condemn the dialectal *wif;* again, such a reaction would betray a lack of understanding of language function. It should be remembered that so-called poor articulation and poor enunciation have little to do with reading success and failure or with anything we might consider to be normal language use. No normal person in normal conversation "talks like a book" clearly enunciating every sound. We all know how tiresome it is to converse with people who over-enunciate in situations calling for a relaxed speech style. A pronunciation such as *wif* is at most a symptom of, say, either a minor pathological defect or a dialect difference; and in either case it is the cause that should be treated, not the symptom. Such treatment may be considered worthwhile only if the particular pathological cause can be remedied or if it is considered desirable to make a standard dialect available to the speaker.

The teaching of reading should take place within a total language program in which reading instruction plays an important part. This total program should emphasize the discovery of how language is used, rather than prescribe how language should be used, as most programs do at present. There are at least two good reasons for such a change in emphasis. First, the discovery approach conforms better to good linguistic, psychological, and pedagogical principles than a prescriptive approach. Second, understanding a process is likely to lead to better use of that process, but only if that understanding has been arrived at in a meaningful way rather than by rote. Language in all its diversity of forms and uses is a fascinating subject for study and can provide a wealth of meaningful exploratory experiences for students of all ages. Children are naturally inquisitive, and it is just as valuable for them to explore their linguistic environment as it is to explore the surrounding fields and woods or streets and stores. Such exploration is likely to be very useful to the child as he begins to understand his linguistic environment, to discover its possibilities, and to use what he finds to further his own ends.

The actual finding-out process should make use of various types of experiences and strategies, so that the teaching is eclectic rather than stereotyped. There are all too many gimmicks and panaceas in existence today in the form of simple solutions to what are essentially complicated problems. Children are different, teachers are different, language has many different facets to it. There is no one royal road to learning; more likely there are a great many paths, few of which are very straight. Children require a variety of linguistic experiences resulting in a variety of effects according to their needs and abilities. Language is uniform and consistent only in the abstract forms described in books by linguists; in real life language is extremely diverse, just as the people who use it are very different. Students cannot learn to savor this diversity if the curriculum offers each student exactly the same linguistic diet.

CHAPTER TEN

Some Implications for Education

If one is prepared to accept a good part of what has been said so far in this book on the subject of reading, then it follows that he must be prepared to accept the need for certain changes in the way that the tasks of teaching reading and of studying the teaching process are usually approached. These changes are of various kinds and are concerned with all aspects of the tasks: research, teacher training, course construction, text writing, and so on. There are obvious implications for all research in reading, since central to such research is the knowledge of language that researchers bring to bear, and any change in researchers' perspective on language will inevitably result in a change in research emphases. Teachers too will have to acquire new understanding and new skills; the kind of training given to potential teachers and to teachers presently in service will have to be reconsidered. Finally, those who are responsible for planning curricula and writing textbooks will have to incorporate in them new content, new approaches to content, and new ideas about learning.

A massive amount of research in reading has been carried out in the last sixty years. Educators have been eager to do research in an attempt to make the study of education if not a "hard" science like chemistry or physics at least a "soft" one like psychology or sociology. They have taken over all the research apparatus of the social sciences: the questionnaires, the surveys, and the controlled studies. Statistical validation of hypotheses has become extremely sophisticated, and even the clinics of the medical practitioner and the laboratories of the "hard" scientist have found a place in educational research. Perhaps nowhere in education are all these more in evidence than in reading research. There is nothing inherently unsound in taking a scientific approach to problems in education in general and to problems in reading in particular; however, the results of such an approach have been rather disappointing, especially in reading, even though one need not be quite so negative about them as Diack (1965).

For one reason or another, however, most of the research in reading is less valuable than it should be. Some research is statistically unsound, but unsoundness of this kind is rapidly disappearing as more and more researchers become familiar with statistics and use the resources of computing centers. A more serious criticism is that most investigators of reading problems have not been aware of basic facts about sound-symbol relationships, about English grammar, about the course of language development in children, and so on. Therefore, while the methodology of the research has often been sound, its content has been less than sound. Subtle and powerful experimental designs are wasted when the underlying hypotheses are based on either false or inadequate views of language. Even today there are disputes about basic facts, and there will always be such disputes, but that should not excuse a serious researcher from using the best linguistic knowledge available when he conducts a piece of research.

The development of modern American linguistics and, more recently, of generative-transformational theory has resulted in an unprecedented level of understanding of linguistic processes and relationships. Unfortunately, this understanding is largely confined to linguists themselves. There has also been considerable ferment within the discipline of linguistics, particularly in the last few years. The Bloomfieldians, having succeeded in their revolution, are now being attacked—routed, some might even say—by the new revolutionaries, the generative-transformationalists. The result is confusion within linguistics and uncertainty without, a situation which has led some educators and teachers to a kind of disenchantment with linguistics. In a few cases this disenchantment is not surprising. More than one linguist in the 1950's seemed ready to promise teachers the answers to all their problems, but such answers never came. The generative-transformationalists themselves for the most part have not yet come down from the mountain bearing tablets with the rules needed to produce improvement in students' language rather than to increase students' interest in language—two very different things— or to help teachers understand the tasks they face in teaching reading, spelling, composition, and so on. But rather than "a plague on you" to linguists for their apparently contradictory statements and preoccupation with theory, teachers and researchers should see current linguistics as an exciting area developing, like science, in fits and starts and by revolution as much as by evolution (Kuhn, 1962). They would be unwise to reject linguistics because of its very strengths rather than because of any weaknesses it might have.

The books and journals commonly available to reading teachers and teaching researchers in general display a low level of familiarity with linguistics. In professional books on reading, in reading journals, and at meetings of reading teachers there is little evidence of any but the most superficial knowledge of linguistics. Linguistics tends to be treated as part of the gimmickry of reading, just another passing fad, so that talks and articles entitled "The use of linguistics in beginning reading instruction" are put on a par with others entitled "The use of the tape recorder in beginning reading instruction." Surveys of the literature are often equally superficial, failing to differentiate between studies that exhibit a serious concern for linguistic findings and insights and those that refer to linguistics only in an attempt to appear up to date. Linguistics is "in," and there is a tendency to use the term *linguistics* loosely, without serious regard for the consequences.

While much linguistic research has been done that could be applied to reading, such as research into phoneme-grapheme correspondences, English syntax, language development in children, and dialects, a great deal still remains to be done, much needs to be done again, and at least some studies would be worth reinterpreting. The notion of the competence-performance distinction requires much further exploration. How does linguistic competence develop in a child, and how is this competence mirrored in performance? What would a theory of reading competence and one of reading performance be like? What really is meant by reading competence, and how does it relate to the competence that writers of generative-transformational grammars attempt to characterize? Some answers have already been proposed to such questions as these, but so far they are extremely tentative.

In addition to the information now available on phoneme-grapheme correspondences, further information on morphophonemic-graphemic correspondences is required, and further exploration of the psychological reality of the morphophoneme is called for. Sapir, a contemporary of Bloomfield, continually hinted at the psychological reality of such a linguistic unit; for example, his untutored Indian informants would insist on making distinctions in writing that Sapir could not hear, and he came to realize that they were required by what we would call morphophonemic rather than phonemic considerations. The morphophoneme, or systematic phoneme as it is sometimes called, is needed in the generative-transformationalist model of competence, but how such a model relates to actual linguistic performance is still very unclear. Relate it must, but while linguists themselves are still debating the validity of such distinctions as competence vs. performance and deep structure vs. surface structure, it would be premature to make a categorical statement that would almost certainly turn out to be wrong. The problem can be illustrated by a rather simple example. In a generative-transformational grammar the letter *a* in **able** and **ability** and **nation** and **national** (the first *a* only) represents the same morphophoneme. It is not clear, however, whether this "sameness" is actually a *psychological* sameness. And even if there is such a psychological sameness, it is not clear how a native speaker of English uses his "knowledge" of that sameness in working out the "correct" pronunciation of each of the four words. It is extremely doubtful that the psychological units and processes available to him are exactly like those that the generative-transformationalists require in order to write their grammars; however, from what we know at present, the psychological units and processes appear to resemble such linguistic units and processes more than they resemble any other units or processes previously discovered or postulated by linguists or psychologists. The temptation is great, therefore, to say that indeed these *are* the actual units and processes; fortunately, some linguists have been more resistant than others to making such claims.

Further research is also needed in dialects. Current studies in dialect variation in several large cities in the United States are having interesting consequences for linguistic theory, particularly in connection with the notion of dialect itself—that is, the notion of what actually constitutes a dialect as opposed to an idiolect on the one hand and a language on the other—and with the idea of linguistic change. Dialect is largely independent of *register*, the way an individual responds in a particular circumstance by adopting a style of speaking appropriate to the subject and the total context. Register itself deserves thorough study because it is an important variable in the classroom and in interpersonal relationships, such as the relationship between reader and author. Teachers generally do not have an adequate understanding of differences among registers and dialects, particularly among nonstandard dialects. Children who speak nonstandard dialects are often said to be deficient in listening and speaking skills, in vocabulary, and even in interests. In reality they are linguistically different, rather than linguistically deficient. Teacher and researchers should reflect this fact in their work.

Another interesting area worth investigating is the ability of a speaker to adjust to another person's speech. We are nearly always able to talk to complete strangers who speak our language, even in difficult circumstances such as over a bad telephone connection, at a noisy street corner, or on a windy day. Human beings seem to have a capacity for adjusting almost instantaneously to the requirements of a particular communication channel. It would appear that we use this same ability when we read, because the reader is able to switch communication channels instantaneously from an auditory to a visual one and from a spoken dialect to a written one and then, as the material he is reading changes, from a reading task of one kind to one of another kind. The existence of this ability provides additional support for the argument that speakers of any dialect of English should be taught to read with books employing the usual printed variety of English. What such speakers need to acquire above all is the ability to choose the appropriate processing technique required for a particular reading task.

Child language itself deserves further investigation, particularly those aspects that relate to the acquisition and development of linguistic competence. As Mussen (1963) has pointed out:

The process of language acquisition is not yet fully understood. . . . It is obviously strongly influenced by environmental conditions and learning. Yet many linguists feel that learning theory cannot fully explain the complex, amazing, and often extremely rapid development of the child's vocabulary and mastery of grammatical structure and semantics. (p. 41)

One psycholinguist, Fodor (1966), has gone even further in criticizing much of the work by psychologists in language learning as follows:

If it be said that the learning-theoretic accounts of reference [that] psychologists have proposed have only been intended as a first step, it must be replied that they are quite certainly a first step in the wrong direction. (p. 110)

Too many studies by psychologists of "language learning" or "linguistic behavior" have been confined to simple frequency counts of sounds, words, and structures in children's language, either at a particular point in time or over a period of time. There is nothing inherently wrong with such counts, because frequency is important, but it is not the only factor to be considered. The range of use of a linguistic unit, the contrastive use of that unit, and significant changes in use over a period of time are more interesting.

Recent studies by Strickland (1962) and Loban (1963, 1966) making use of linguistic insights into language description and language function show a beginning being made in identifying the developmental patterns and diversity of children's language and in relating them to non-linguistic factors. One point made by Strickland is of special interest:

The oral language children use is far more advanced than the language of the books in which they are taught to read. Perhaps this is as it should be, but evidence is needed as to whether children would be aided or hindered by the use of sentences in their books more like the sentences they use in their speech. (p. 106)

As we have seen in previous chapters, the language of writing and the language of speech are different; the precise relationship of skills in one to skills in the other needs further study. Many people, including some linguists, have assumed a close relationship, but we may eventually find that no such close relationship exists and that there are critically important differences between the two sets of skills. It may not even be possible to give an adequate definition of *skills* in this sense. Fluency, knowledge of frequencies, control of grammar, variety, resourcefulness—all of these are skills, just as the ability to link speech and writing is a skill. But to understand these skills one must understand what language is, and at best one can offer only an inadequate account of the latter.

Reading teachers therefore need a much better understanding of language than, in general, they presently exhibit. However, linguistic sophistication cannot be acquired by reading a chapter or two in a textbook, or by listening to a few lectures, or even by attending a two-week crash course. A solid mastery of linguistics requires extensive course work, much reading, and time to think. Reading teachers must learn to cease perpetuating the old myths and falsehoods. For example, they must learn how to take advantage of the systematic nature of English spelling, how to view problems of nonstandard dialect and usage with intelligence and sensitivity, and how to avoid normative judgments in favor of descriptive statements. Teachers can clarify their understanding of the relationship of speech to writing. They might also do well to consider the following statement by Cohn (1959) about types of speech which vary from the norm of standard English:

> We fear lower-class speech and are inclined to give it no quarter. The more precarious our social status in the higher classes—that is, the closer we are to the line that divides the middle from the lower classes or the more recent our ascent from the lower strata—the more insistent we are on the purity of our linguistic credentials. Such insecurity is perhaps especially troublesome to public school teachers, whose separation from the lower classes is often recent and precarious. (p. 439)

Teachers quite often fill a peculiar position in society, one that sometimes creates uncertainty and even pain for them. They should therefore be prepared to examine their attitudes towards language as well as the state of their knowledge of language.

Teachers of reading should be interested in the varieties of linguistic behavior that surround them in the classroom and in the larger society. They should view their task of teaching reading, which is one variety of linguistic behavior, within the wider context of total language behavior. Language arts programs should offer both teachers and students the opportunity to explore their linguistic environment as an entity, rather than compartmentalizing the various language activities into spelling, handwriting, reading, composition, literature, and so on. Such programs should not be based on any single psychological learning theory. In the absence of any clearly defined theory as to how language skills are acquired and how children learn, and in the knowledge that different students bring different abilities and interests to their learning tasks, it would seem wiser to be eclectic. At the same time the current notion of inquiry, of allowing students to pursue their own interests, to ask their own questions, and to try to find answers that work for them, seems ideally suited to a language curriculum that has as its goal the development of integrated linguistic behavior.

Such a curriculum requires a new kind of textbook. Beginning reading materials should be made to conform to what we know about children's language and about language in general, as should teacher-training guides, manuals, and texts, many of which are no less unsound or misleading. Statements about language should be based on our current knowledge of linguistic behavior and the structure of language, and they should be included only when necessary and appropriate to the teaching task. Particulary worthy of re-examination are the long lists of generalizations that students are supposed to acquire in reading: their inaccuracy is perhaps only exceeded by their vagueness. The role of generalization in reading, particularly that of phonic generalizations, needs to be re-examined.

There are at least four principles that good materials and methods for teaching reading must observe:

1. They must be based on sound linguistic content, on the best available descriptions of language and of the English language in particular, rather than on random collections of myths.
2. They must be based on a thorough understanding of how children "know" their language as this knowledge reveals itself in what they can do in their language, rather than in what they can verbalize about their language.
3. They must differentiate between the descriptive and the pre-

scriptive, particularly when the prescriptions are unrealistic. When the prescriptions refer to standard English, the methods and materials should reflect some decision about the relationship (if any) between teaching reading and teaching a standard spoken dialect.

4. Finally, they must recognize the important active contribution the learner makes in reading, both in trying to make sense of the orthographic patterns of English and in trying to make sense out of sentences. Too often teachers seek to reward the learner's correct responses and, in one way or another, to punish his incorrect ones. Good methods and materials should also focus on these incorrect responses, because they can tell us just as much as we will let them tell us.

A good language arts curriculum, adequate texts, and well-prepared teachers should produce students who will be able to read well and who at the same time will have a more realistic and inquiring attitude towards language and linguistic problems than the one that currently prevails. Today's educated readers read well, to be sure, but they have little idea about the function of language in their lives and little tolerance for linguistic deviance from an artificial norm. Too often their use of language is inhibited by the restrictions imposed by well-intentioned but linguistically ill-informed teachers and scholars. Reading taught from a linguistic perspective should allow future generations both to read more proficiently and enjoyably and to use their language in its full vigor and richness.

GLOSSARY

allomorph A positional variant of a morpheme. The endings of *cats*, *dogs*, and *churches* all have the same meaning "plural" but they are different phonemically (/s/~/z/~/əz/) and are therefore allomorphs of the "plural" morpheme.

allophone A positional variant of a phoneme. The initial sound in *pin* [pʻ] and the second sound in *spin* [p] are phonetically different, but this difference is quite predictable in English and never results in a difference in meaning; it is therefore an allophonic difference, not a phonemic one.

alphabet A writing system for a language in which there is a correspondence between the phonemes of the language and the symbols in the orthography.

anaphora Reference to something that has already been mentioned, often through a process of substitution. For example, *did too* in *I said it and he did too* avoids the repetition of *said it*.

articulation Alterations of the various cavities and passages of the vocal tract to produce the sounds of speech.

aspect A marking of a verb to indicate whether an action is beginning, completed, in progress, repetitive, and so on, such as the progressive aspect of *They are running.*

aspiration A puff of air accompanying the release of a consonant, as with the initial consonants of English *pin, tin,* and *kin.*

auxiliary A verb that combines with another verb to form a phrase; for example, *have* in *have gone* or *can* in *can go.*

backed Produced in a position further back in the mouth than what may be regarded as the basic position of the sound. The *c* of *cool* is backed in comparison with the *c* of *calm.*

brackets The symbols used to enclose phonetic notation: [   ].

checked vowel   The vowel in a closed syllable (a syllable ending in a consonant), as in *at, get, ape,* and *bite.* The English vowels in *at* and *get* can occur only in closed syllables, so these are always checked; those in *ape* and *bite* may also occur unchecked (free), as in *gay* and *my.*

citation form   A linguistic form pronounced in isolation; for example, *have* rather than the *'ve* of *I could've gone.*

closed syllable   A syllable ending in one or more consonant sounds; for example, *cat, bump, apt,* and *strength.*

code   A set of symbols used to represent a system. For example, the English alphabet may be regarded as a code that represents the English phonemic system, and Morse Code as a code that represents the English alphabet in another medium.

collocation   The likelihood that two or more words will occur in the same environment; for example, *car, road,* and *drive.*

competence   The ability of native speakers to form and understand grammatical sentences, detect deviant and ungrammatical sentences, and make other linguistic judgments about utterances in their language.

complementary distribution   The occurrence of variants of a linguistic unit in different environments. Two or more linguistic variants are in complementary distribution when they have no common environment; for example, the "plural" allomorphic variants /s/ of *cats* and /z/ of *dogs,* and the /p/ allophonic variants [p'] in *pin* [p'ɪn] and [p] in *spin* [spɪn].

complementation   The structural relationship between a verb and its complement(s), as in *took/the book, gave/him/a dollar,* and *wanted/to go.*

complex sentence   A sentence containing an embedded sentence, such as *He left when I arrived,* which contains a main sentence and a subordinated (embedded) sentence.

consonant   A sound formed by constriction of the air stream in the vocal tract; also a letter to symbolize such a sound.

constituent parts   The parts of a grammatical construction, as in *two/books, slept/in, He left/when I left, over/the moon.*

constituent structure   A grammatical construction, usually consisting of two parts but occasionally of three.

coordination   The structural relationship between two grammatical units joined by *and, but, or,* etc., as in *bread and butter, very tired but extremely happy,* and *We'll sink or swim.*

deep structure   The abstract structure postulated as underlying a sentence. It contains all the information necessary for the semantic interpretation of that sentence.

deep subject   The noun phrase that is the subject of a deep structure and that may or may not become the surface subject. In *Jim kicked Tom* and *Tom was kicked by Jim, Jim* is the deep subject of both sentences but the surface subject of only the first sentence.

deictic word   A "pointing" word, such as *this, that, here, there.*

derivation   A process by which non-inflectional affixes are added to bases to form words, as in *government, hopeful, distrustful.*

deviant or nonsense sentence   A sentence that appears strange or unusual to a native speaker for semantic reasons; for example, *Colorless green ideas sleep furiously. The fishes spoke square apples.*

dialect   The variety of a language spoken in a particular area (regional dialect) or by a particular group of speakers (social dialect).

differential meaning   The meaning difference that must exist when two utterances are not repetitions. *He killed a cat* and *He killed a rat* show minimal differential meaning.

discourse   A group of sentences related in some sequential manner.

distribution   The set of environments in which a particular linguistic form may appear.

dummy element   An element that must be postulated to exist at the level of deep structure so that certain characteristics of surface structure may be explained. For example, the elements *IM-PERATIVE you* and *will* in the deep structure *IMPERATIVE you will go,* which underlies the actual sentence *Go!*

economy   The principle that states that given two explanations that account for a given body of data, the briefer one is the better one.

embedded sentence   A sentence that is included in another sentence, as *(when) I arrived* is embedded in *He left when I arrived.*

eye dialect   The practice of suggesting a nonstandard dialect by changing the standard spelling forms of words that both standard and nonstandard speakers pronounce in the manner suggested by the changed forms; for example, *wuz* for *was* and *I could of* for *I could've.*

final pitch contour   The movement of the pitch of the voice (up, level, down) at the end of an utterance. Compare *He left yesterday.* (↓) with *He left yesterday?* (↑) and *He left yesterday* (→), *I said* (↓).

final position   Before a pause, as are *t* in *cat,* [t] in [kˈæt], *man* in *postman,* and *outside* in *He's outside.*

finite system   A system employing a limited number of units and rules.

form class   A set of words that take a certain set of affixes. English nouns take a plural suffix *(cats)* and a possessive suffix *(cat's)*, verbs take a past tense suffix *(baked)* and participle suffixes *(baked, baking)*, and adjectives take a comparative suffix *(wiser)* and a superlative suffix *(wisest)*.

formative   An element in the deep structure of a sentence; for example, *QUESTION, SOMEONE, past,* and *leave* in *QUESTION SOMEONE past leave (Who left?)*.

fragment   A portion of a sentence.

free form   A linguistic form that can occur as an independent word, like *cat, judge,* and *happy* but not the *s* of *cats,* the *ment* of *judgment,* or the *un* of *unhappy.*

free vowel   A vowel that may appear in an open syllable—that is, a syllable that does not end in a consonant—such as the vowels in *may, see,* and *sue.* (Note that these same vowels frequently occur in English in closed syllables, as in *made, seed,* and *suit.*)

fronted   Produced in a position further forward in the mouth than what may be regarded as the basic position of the sound. The *c* of *cat* is fronted in comparison with the *c* of *calm.*

generative grammar   A grammar that assigns structural descriptions to sentences, enabling us to say what the constituents are and what the relationships are among them. A complete generative grammar for a language would do this for all the grammatical sentences of the language.

generative-transformational grammar   A grammar that assigns structural descriptions to sentences and relates the deep structures and meanings of those sentences to their surface structures and sounds.

grammar   The possible arrangements of words in a language.

grammatical   Accepted by native speakers as a possible arrangement of words in a language.

grammatical marking   The inflecting of words according to form class. For example, a certain set of English words may be classified as nouns because they all can be marked for "plural": *cat, cats; dog, dogs; church, churches; man, men.*

graphology   The written forms of language.

homophones   Two or more words with identical pronunciations but different meanings: (1) *He bores me.* (2) *He hunted boars.* (3) *It bores a hole in wood.* Homophones may also be homographs, as in (1) and (3), when there is no spelling distinction.

ideograph   A symbol that represents an idea or concept.

idiolect   The speech characteristic of an individual.

immediate constituents   The parts, usually two, of a construction, as *house* and *wife* are the immediate constituents (or IC's) of *housewife, Birds* and *sing* the IC's of *Birds sing,* and *un* and *happy* the IC's of *unhappy.*

inflection   An affix (in English, usually a suffix) that changes the form of a word without changing its form class or basic meaning: *cat* and *man* may be inflected for "plural" *(cats, men)* or possessive *(cat's, man's)* or both *(cats', men's).*

intonation contour or pattern   The pattern of rising and/or falling pitches with which a sentence is pronounced.

inversion   A change in what may be considered as the normal declarative word order, as in *Are you happy? (You are happy)* and *Never have I seen such foolishness (I have never seen such foolishness).* In the first case the inversion is required by the grammatical rules of English; in the second it is a stylistic or rhetorical device.

irregular   Not conforming to the general rule. *Men* is an irregular English noun plural and *sang* an irregular past tense. Regular forms would have been °*mans* and °*singed* (compare *pans* and *winged).*

kernel sentence   A term used in earlier versions of generative-transformational grammar to describe active, positive, and declarative sentences from which passive, negative, imperative, and interrogative sentences could be derived.

Latinate grammar   A grammatical description of a language using principles and a terminology derived from descriptions of Latin.

lax   Pronounced with very little muscular tension in the articulators; for example, [z] is lax, whereas [s] is tense.

lexical   Referring to the words of a language.

lexicon   The total set of morphemes and words in a language.

logograph   A symbol that represents a unit of meaning, such as a morpheme, rather than a unit of sound, such as a phoneme.

"long" vowel   For many reading teachers, a vowel that says its own name, that is the vowels in *safe, cede, sign, hope,* and *fuse.*

low-level phonological rule   A rule that specifies some relatively unimportant phonetic characteristic of the pronunciation of a phoneme; for example, that in English a nasal consonant must also be voiced, or an initial voiceless stop must also be aspirated.

mentalism   The use of invented data rather than observed data and of a native speaker's reaction to data rather than actual responses to sentences. On the other hand, antimentalism refers to the use of observed data rather than invented data and of actual responses rather than responses about responses.

minimal pair   Two utterances distinguished by a single contrast, like *pat/bat; It's a battle/It's a bottle;* and *He's ready/He's ready?*

modal   An auxiliary verb such as *can, shall, will,* and *may* (and their past tense forms, *could, should, would,* and *might).*

modification   The relationship between a head (H) and a modifier (M), as in *old/man* (MH), *sit/down* (HM), and *the man/in the moon* (HM).

morpheme   A minimal unit of meaning. Both *cat* and *s* in *cats* are morphemes.

morphophoneme   A phonological unit corresponding to a set of phonemes that occurs within the allomorphs of a particular morpheme: the distribution of the set of phonemes in the morphophoneme is explicable in terms of phonological environments. For example, the //s// morphophoneme of the English plural is predictably realized by three sibilants (s~z~əz) according to the final phoneme of the noun to which it is attached (c<u>at</u>, do<u>g</u>, chur<u>ch</u>).

nasal   Produced by the release of air through the nose. The *m, n,* and *ng* of *Pam, pan,* and *pang* are nasal consonants.

natural language   A language spoken naturally by human beings, in contrast to the artificial languages of computers, mathematics, and symbolic logic, or languages like Esperanto, or the communication systems of other species.

neutralization   The absence of a contrast between two phonemes in a particular phonological environment: /i/ and /iy/ contrast before most consonants, for example in *bit* and *beat,* but not before /r/, so *here* may be written as either /hir/ or /hiyr/, or even with a special symbol (an archiphoneme) as /hɪr/.

nonsense syllable   A syllable pattern that is not used in a language but is nevertheless possible, like *gleat, bimp,* and *shromp,* as opposed to an impossible syllable like *ngleikz.*

non-significant   Not resulting in a difference in meaning.

nonstandard English   A dialect diverging noticeably from a standard dialect in pronunciation, lexicon, and/or grammar.

open syllable   A syllable ending in a vowel sound; for example, *be, they,* and *sigh.*

orthography   A spelling system.

pause   A significant break in a stream of sound: compare the placing of the pauses in *Nye trait* and *nightrate* with the lack of pause in *nitrate.*

performance   The actual utterances produced by speakers of a language.

phoneme   A significant contrastive unit in the phonological system of a language.

phoneme-grapheme correspondence   The relationship between a contrastive sound unit (phoneme) and a contrastive alphabetic unit (grapheme or letter), as, for example, between an English phoneme /æ/ and its usual grapheme correspondent *a*, or between /č/ and *ch* or *tch.*

phonemic notation   A system for recording the phonemes of a language. The notation is written within diagonal bars: *cat* is written as /kæt/ and *high* as /hay/ in one well-known system of phonemic notation.

phonemic principle   The principle that the sound system of a language is composed of a set of significant contrastive units or phonemes.

phonemics   The procedures for establishing the phonemes of a language; also, the resulting system.

phonetic   Referring to language sounds.

phonetic features   Features of sounds such as voice, stop quality, vowel quality, and nasality.

phonetic notation or system   A transcriptional system used to record all noticeable phonetic features.

phonetic representation   The pronunciation of a particular linguistic form.

phonetic similarity   The sharing of at least one phonetic feature by two or more sounds, as [m] and [b] share the feature "bilabial" and [b] and [d] the feature "stop."

phonetic variant   One of the possible pronunciations of a phoneme: a positional variant or allophone.

phonetics   The study of the production, transmission, and reception of language sounds.

phonic generalization   A rule for the pronunciation of a particular grapheme or combination of graphemes, for example "a *c* before an *e* or an *i* usually is pronounced [s]" or "when two vowels occur together, usually the second is silent and the first has its long sound."

phonics   A way of teaching reading in which children are taught the relationships of symbols to sounds.

phonology   A cover term for both phonetics and phonemics.

phrase structure grammar   A grammar that describes the grammatical structures of sentences without the use of transformations.

pitch   The height of the voice. It varies during the production of English sentences in systematic ways.

positional variant   A variant of a phoneme (allophone) or morpheme (allomorph) occurring in a specific environment. The phoneme [t] has a [tʻ] allophone initially in *top* but a [t] allophone after *s* in *stop;* one English negative morpheme has an /in/ allomorph in *intolerant* (before /t/), an /im/ allomorph in *impossible* (before /p/), and an /i/ allomorph in *illegible* (before /l/).

possible word   A word that conforms to the phonemic and grammatical patterns of the language but that has no meaning (or is nonsensical); for example, *stopes* and *glink* in *Do stopes glink?*

predicate phrase   The part of a sentence containing the verb and any complements it may have.

predication   The relationship between a subject noun phrase and a predicate phrase: *John/says, The man/left the room,* and *Little Jack Horner/sat in the corner.*

prefix   An affix placed before the morpheme or morphemes to which it is attached: *intolerant, dishonor,* and *reflect.*

prescriptivism   The doctrine that part of the grammarian's task is to prescribe good usage in order to improve the language.

productive inflection   An inflection used for newly coined words. For example, *one sputnik, two sputniks.*

projection rules   A set of rules for combining the meanings of the individual words of a sentence into a possible meaning for the whole sentence.

pronominal   A word that can replace a noun phrase: *The old man/left. He/left.*

pronominalization   The transformation that substitutes a pronominal for a noun phrase: *John hurt John* is pronominalized to *John hurt himself* if only one person is involved.

psycholinguistics   The study of the interrelationships of psychological and linguistic behavior.

recursiveness   The capability of infinite expansion: *This is the dog that worried the cat that killed the rat that ate the malt that lay in the house that Jack built.*

reflex   An observable datum for which a historical or abstract explanation may be provided. The spelling *night* is a reflex of what we know to be a much different pronunciation in Middle English. The *you* of *Behave yourself* is a reflex of a deep structure containing *you,* such as *You will behave.*

register   A variety of a language characteristic of a certain kind of user: surgeons, airplane pilots, gamblers, and stamp collectors all use different registers of English.

regular   Conforming to the general pattern: *cats* is a regular plural whereas *men* is irregular.

root   A morpheme that can occur with various other morphemes to form different words but always retains its meaning: *joy* in *joys, joyful,* and *enjoy.*

rule   A formal statement which relates one grammatical unit to another.

semantics   The study of meaning.

semantic properties   The component meanings of a morpheme or word. Part of the meaning of *cat,* for example, is that it is "animal," "non-human," and "concrete."

sentence   An arrangement of words for which a structural description is provided by a grammar.

sentence compounding   The conjoining of two or more sentences by a word such as *and* or *but.*

sentence patterns   Patterns such as Noun+Verb+Noun that may be used to characterize the structures of sentences. *Birds sing* is Noun+Verb and *The man gave his friend a dollar* is $Noun^1$+Verb+$Noun^2$+$Noun^3$. (The superscripts 1, 2, 3, refer to the fact that the nouns have different referents.)

"short" vowel   For many reading teachers, a vowel that does not "say its own name" and that cannot appear in an open syllable; for example, the vowels of *bit, bet, bat,* and *but.*

sibilant   An *s*-like sound. The middle consonants in *passing, fizzing, fishing,* and *measure* are sibilants.

significant   Resulting in a difference in meaning in certain circumstances.

simple sentence   A sentence containing only one finite verb—that is, only one verb marked for tense.

slot-filler correlation   The relationship between part of a linguistic structure and the type of unit that can function in that part; for example, a noun may fill a subject function or slot in a subject-predicate construction.

Standard English   A dialect spoken (and written) by a prestige group in society and usually lacking noticeable local characteristics.

stop   A consonantal sound made by completely blocking the airstreams: *pole, toll, coal, bowl, dole,* and *goal* all begin with stops.

stress   The relative intensity with which a vowel is pronounced. Compare the different intensities of the vowels in *the man* or *the*

old greenhouse. These differences are usually quite predictable for native speakers.

string A sequence of formatives or morphemes in a sentence.

subordination The relationship between a dependent element and an independent element in a grammatical structure. In the sentence *He was there when I left,* the clause *I left* is subordinated to *He was there* by means of the subordinator *when.*

suffix A morpheme placed at the end of the morpheme or morphemes to which it is attached. The *s* in *cats* is an inflectional suffix, whereas the *ment* in *judgment* is a derivational one.

suprasegmental phonemes The phonemes of stress, pitch, and pause.

surface structure The relationships among the words of an actually observed sentence.

syllabary A writing system whose basic units represent syllables.

syllabic Referring to syllables.

syllabication The process of dividing words into syllables.

syllable A unit of the phonological system with a vowel as its nucleus.

symmetrical patterning The principle that languages tend to have symmetrical sound systems. Thus, if a language has four voiceless stops contrasting with each other and also a set of voiced stops contrasting with these voiceless ones, this voiced set is also likely to number four.

syntax The arrangements of words in a language into grammatical sequences.

systematic phonemes The phonemes of a language as analyzed by a generative-transformational linguist.

taxonomic phonemes The phonemes of a language as analyzed by a structural linguist. They are established by using either minimal pairs or the principles of complementary distribution and phonetic similarity. The taxonomic phonemic system is established independently of the grammatical and semantic systems according to a set of well-defined procedures.

tense Pronounced with noticeable muscular tension in the articulators; for example, [s] is tense, whereas [z] is lax.

tense element The English "non-past" or "past" tense. A finite English verb is either "non-past" or "past" in tense, "non-past" as in *I think, you bake,* and *he sings* and "past" as in *I thought, you baked,* and *he sang.*

transformation In grammar, one of the processes by which a deep structure is turned into a surface structure; in phonology, one of the processes by which a surface structure is turned into phonetic output.

unaspirated   Having no accompanying puff of air, like the *t* of *stop* as opposed to the aspirated *t* of *top*.

ungrammatical   Not generated by the grammar and/or not produced by native speakers. Ungrammatical forms are usually preceded by an asterisk in the writings of linguists: *°He no come. °Come you the garden into.*

universal grammarians   Those seventeenth- and eighteenth-century grammarians who stressed the similarities of languages rather than the ways in which languages vary.

universals   Grammatical features found in all languages.

utterance   A spoken sentence.

vocal   Realized in sounds.

voiced   Produced with vibration of the vocal cords, like the initial sounds in *vat, big, then, nose,* and *ape*.

voiceless   Produced with no vibration of the vocal cords, like the initial sounds in *fat, pig,* and *thin*.

voicing   With accompanying vibration of the vocal cords.

vowel   A sound produced by the vibration of the vocal cords and allowed an unobstructed passage through the mouth; also, a letter to symbolize such a sound.

vowel reduction   A change in vowel quality in certain environments, as, for example, under weak stress. Compare the vowels in *man* and *postman;* in *men* and *postmen;* and in *Canada* and *Canadian.*

well-formed   Capable of being assigned a structural description.

word   A morpheme or combination of morphemes that is regarded as a pronounceable and meaningful unit.

word boundary   The pause that marks the end of a word.

BIBLIOGRAPHY

BAILEY, MILDRED H., "The Utility of Phonic Generalizations in Grades One Through Six." *Reading Teacher*, Vol. 20 (1967), pp. 413–18.

BECKER, ALTON L., "A Tagmemic Approach to Paragraph Analysis." *College Composition and Communication*, Vol. 16 (1965), pp. 237–42.

BERLYNE, D. E., "Recent Developments in Piaget's Work." *British Journal of Educational Psychology*, Vol. 27 (1957), pp. 1–12.

BERNSTEIN, BASIL, "Elaborated and Restricted Codes: Their Social Origins and Some Consequences," in J. J. Gumperz and Dell Hymes, eds., "The Ethnography of Communication." *American Anthropologist Special Publication*, 66:2 (1964), pp. 55–69.

BERNSTEIN, BASIL, "Elaborated and Restricted Codes: An Outline," in Stanley Lieberson, ed., "Explorations in Sociolinguistics." *International Journal of American Linguistics*, 33:4 (1967), Part 2, pp. 126–33.

BETTS, EMMETT A., "Linguistics and Reading." *Education*, Vol. 86 (1966), pp. 454–58.

BLOOMFIELD, LEONARD, "Why a Linguistic Society?" *Language*, Vol. 1 (1925), pp. 1–5.

BLOOMFIELD, LEONARD, "Literate and Illiterate Speech." *American Speech*, Vol. 2 (1927), pp. 432–39.

BLOOMFIELD, LEONARD, and CLARENCE L. BARNHART, *Let's Read*. Detroit, Wayne State University Press, 1961.

BURMEISTER, LOU E., "Usefulness of Phonic Generalizations." *Reading Teacher*, Vol. 21 (1968), pp. 349–56, 360.

CARROLL, JOHN B., "The Analysis of Reading Instruction: Perspectives from Psychology and Linguistics," in E. R. Hilgard, ed., *Theories of Learning and Instruction*, N.S.S.E. 63rd Yearbook, Part 1. Chicago, University of Chicago Press, 1964a, Chapter 14.

CARROLL, JOHN B., *Language and Thought*. Englewood Cliffs, N.J., Prentice-Hall, 1964b.

CHALL, JEANNE, *Learning to Read: The Great Debate.* New York, McGraw-Hill, 1967.

CHOMSKY, NOAM, *Syntactic Structures.* The Hague, Mouton & Co., 1957.

CHOMSKY, NOAM, "Some Methodological Remarks on Generative Grammar." *Word,* Vol. 17 (1961), pp. 219–39.

CHOMSKY, NOAM, "Comments for Project Literacy Meeting." *Project Literary Reports No. 2* (1964), Cornell University, pp. 1–8.

CHOMSKY, NOAM, *Aspects of the Theory of Syntax.* Cambridge, Mass., MIT Press, 1965.

CHOMSKY, NOAM, *Cartesian Linguistics.* New York, Harper & Row, 1966.

CHOMSKY, NOAM, and MORRIS HALLE, *The Sound Pattern of English.* New York, Harper & Row, 1968.

CLYMER, THEODORE, "The Utility of Phonic Generalizations in the Primary Grades." *Reading Teacher,* Vol. 16 (1963), pp. 252–58.

COHN, WERNER, "On the Language of Lower-Class Children." *School Review,* Vol. 67 (1959), pp. 435–40.

DEVINE, THOMAS G., "Linguistic Research and the Teaching of Reading." *Journal of Reading,* Vol. 9 (1966), pp. 273–77.

DIACK, HUNTER, *The Teaching of Reading, in Spite of the Alphabet.* New York, Philosophical Library, 1965.

DILLARD, J. L., "A New Problem for the Inner City Language Teacher." Unpublished manuscript.

DIXON, ROBERT M. W., *What Is Language? A New Approach to Linguistic Description.* London, Longmans, Green Ltd., 1965.

DURKIN, DOLORES, *Phonics and the Teaching of Reading,* 2nd ed. New York, Teachers College Press, 1965.

EDFELDT, AKE W., *Silent Speech and Silent Reading.* Chicago, University of Chicago Press, 1960.

EMANS, ROBERT, "The Usefulness of Phonic Generalizations Above the Primary Grades." *Reading Teacher,* Vol. 20 (1967), pp. 419–25.

FLESCH, RUDOLPH, *Why Johnny Can't Read—and What You Can Do About It.* New York, Harper & Row, 1955.

FODOR, JERRY A., "How to Learn to Talk: Some Simple Ways," in Frank Smith and George A. Miller, eds., *The Genesis of Language.* Cambridge, Mass., MIT Press, 1966, pp. 105–22.

FRIES, CHARLES C., *Teaching and Learning English as a Foreign Language.* Ann Arbor, University of Michigan Press, 1945.

FRIES, CHARLES C., *The Structure of English.* New York, Harcourt, Brace & World, 1952.

FRIES, CHARLES C., *Linguistics and Reading.* New York, Holt, Rinehart and Winston, 1963.

FRIES, CHARLES C., and AILEEN A. TRAVER, *English Word Lists.* Ann Arbor, George Wahr Publishing Co., 1950.

GATES, ARTHUR I., "Character and Purposes of the Yearbook," in N. B. Henry, ed., *Reading in the Elementary School*, N.S.S.E. 48th Yearbook, Part 2. Chicago, University of Chicago Press, 1949, Chapter 1.

GELB, I. J., *A Study of Writing*, 2nd ed. Chicago, University of Chicago Press, 1963.

GLEASON, H. A., JR., *An Introduction to Descriptive Linguistics*, rev. ed. New York, Holt, Rinehart and Winston, 1961.

GOODMAN, KENNETH S., "The Linguistics of Reading." *Elementary School Journal*, Vol. 64 (1964), pp. 355–61.

GOODMAN, KENNETH S., "Dialect Barriers to Reading Comprehension." *Elementary English*, Vol. 42 (1965), pp. 853–60.

GOODMAN, KENNETH S., "Reading: A Psycholinguistic Guessing Game." Paper presented at the meeting of the American Educational Research Association, New York, February 16, 1967.

HALL, ROBERT A., JR., *Introductory Linguistics*. Philadelphia, Chilton Company, 1964.

HARRISON, MAURICE, *Instant Reading: The Story of the Initial Teaching Alphabet*. London, Sir Isaac Pitman & Sons, Ltd., 1964.

HEILMAN, ARTHUR W., *Phonics in Proper Perspective*. Columbus, Ohio, Charles E. Merrill, 1964.

HILL, KENNETH C., "Some Notes on English Vowel Morphophonemics." *Language Learning*, Vol. 18 (1968), pp. 77–88.

HOCKETT, CHARLES F., *A Course in Modern Linguistics*. New York, Macmillan, 1958.

KATZ, JEROLD J., and JERRY A. FODOR, "The Structure of a Semantic Theory." *Language*, Vol. 39 (1963), pp. 170–210.

KUHN, THOMAS, *The Structure of Scientific Revolutions*. Chicago, University of Chicago Press, 1962.

LABOV, WILLIAM, "Some Sources of Reading Problems for Negro Speakers of Nonstandard English," in A. Frazier, ed., *New Directions in Elementary English*. Champaign, Ill., National Council of Teachers of English, 1967.

LEFEVRE, CARL A., *Linguistics and the Teaching of Reading*. New York, McGraw-Hill, 1964.

LENNEBERG, ERIC H., *Biological Foundations of Language*. New York, Wiley, 1967.

LOBAN, WALTER, *The Language of Elementary School Children*. Champaign, Ill., National Council of Teachers of English, 1963.

LOBAN, WALTER, *Problems in Oral English*. Champaign, Ill., National Council of Teachers of English, 1966.

LYONS, J., and R. J. WALES, eds., *Psycholinguistics Papers: The Proceed-*

ings of the 1966 Edinburgh Conference. Edinburgh, Edinburgh University Press, 1966.

MALINOWSKI, BRONISLAW, "The Problem of Meaning in Primitive Languages," in C. K. Ogden and I. A. Richards, eds., *The Meaning of Meaning.* New York, Harcourt, Brace & World, 1923.

MATHEWS, MITFORD H., *Teaching to Read: Historically Considered.* Chicago, University of Chicago Press, 1966.

MCBRIDE, FERGUS, *Teachers' Course in Writing in i.t.a.* University of London, Institute of Education, Reading Research Document No. 6, 1965.

MILLER, GEORGE A., "The Magical Number Seven, Plus or Minus Two: Some Limits on Our Capacity for Processing Information." *Psychological Review*, Vol. 63 (1956), pp. 81–97.

MUSSEN, PAUL H., *The Psychological Development of the Child.* Englewood Cliffs, N.J., Prentice-Hall, 1963.

NEISSER, ULRIC, *Cognitive Psychology.* New York, Appleton-Century-Crofts, 1967.

NIDA, EUGENE A., *Toward a Science of Translation.* Leiden, E. J. Brill, 1964.

OSGOOD, C. E., G. C. SUCI, and P. H. TANNENBAUM, *The Measurement of Meaning.* Urbana, University of Illinois Press, 1957.

PIKE, KENNETH L., *Phonemics: A Technique for Reducing Languages to Writing.* Ann Arbor, University of Michigan Press, 1947.

PIKE, KENNETH L., "Beyond the Sentence." *College Composition and Communication*, Vol. 15 (1964), pp. 129–35.

POSTAL, PAUL M., "On So-Called 'Pronouns' in English," in Francis P. Dinneen, ed., *Report of the 17th Annual Round Table Meeting on Linguistics and Language Studies.* Washington, D.C., Georgetown University Press, 1966, pp. 177–206.

ROBINSON, HELEN M., *Why Pupils Fail in Reading.* Chicago, University of Chicago Press, 1946.

SHANNON, C. E., and W. WEAVER, *The Mathematical Theory of Communication.* Urbana, University of Illinois Press, 1949.

SHUY, ROGER W., ed., *Social Dialects and Language Learning: Proceedings of the Bloomington, Indiana, Conferences, 1964.* Champaign, Ill., National Council of Teachers of English, 1965.

SHUY, ROGER W., *Discovering American Dialects.* Champaign, Ill., National Council of Teachers of English, 1967.

SMITH, HENRY L., "Review of *Let's Read." Language*, Vol. 39 (1963), pp. 67–78.

SOFFIETTI, JAMES B., "Why Children Fail to Read: A Linguistic Analysis." *Harvard Educational Review*, Vol. 25 (1955), pp. 63–84.

SOUTHGATE, VERA, "Approaching i.t.a. Results with Caution." *Reading Research Quarterly*, 1:3 (1966), pp. 35–56.

SPACHE, GEORGE, *Reading in the Elementary School*. Boston, Allyn and Bacon, 1964.

STEWART, WILLIAM A., "Sociolinguistic Factors in the History of American Negro Dialects." *The Florida FL Reporter*, 5:2 (1967), pp. 1–4.

STRICKLAND, RUTH G., "The Language of Elementary School Children: Its Relationship to the Language of Reading Textbooks and the Quality of Reading of Selected Children." *Bulletin of the School of Education, Indiana University*, 38:4 (1962), whole number.

VENEZKY, RICHARD L., "English Orthography: Its Graphical Structure and Its Relation to Sound." *Reading Research Quarterly*, 2:3 (1967), pp. 75–105.

VYGOTSKY, L. S., *Thought and Language*. Cambridge, Mass., MIT-Wiley, 1962.

WARDHAUGH, RONALD, "Syl-lab-i-ca-tion." *Elementary English*, Vol. 43 (1966), pp. 785–88.

oral reading, 16, 23, 139
orthography, 16, 22, 23, 25–27, 55, 56, 107, 118, 134, 135
Osgood, C. E., 89

paragraphs, 80–82
performance, linguistic, 36–38, 45–46, 50, 58–61, 75, 80, 131, 136, 139–40, 144–45
phatic communion, 80
phoneme-grapheme correspondences, 16, 18–19, 25, 27, 28, 102–07, 133–35, 138
phonemics, 20–21, 26, 32, 33, 35, 99–102, 105, 108
phonetics, 7 8, 21, 32, 99–100
phonic generalizations, 10–11, 117, 149
phonics:
    Bloomfield's criticisms of, 15–17
    misconceptions in, 6–11, 105–06
    phonemics and, 21–22, 105–06
    phonetics and, 7–8, 21, 105 06
    research in, 5 6
phonological rules, 48–49, 114, 127, 130–31
phrase structure grammars, 46, 55
Piaget, Jean, 129–30
Pike, Kenneth L., 80, 99
Pitman, Sir James, 25
Postal, Paul M., 80

readability formulae, 88
reading:
    definition of, 133
    failure in, 2–5
    information processing and, 52–59, 133–34, 137, 146, 150
    linguistic method in, 12–15, 135
    research in, 5–6, 10–12, 21, 28, 30, 142–43
    social adjustment and, 2–3, 5, 19
    teaching methods in, 5–6
recursiveness, 44–46, 73
reference, 65, 84
register, 146
regularity, 86–87, 106, 108–09, 134

resonance theory, 132, 137
restricted codes, 129
rewriting conventions, 39–44
Robinson, Helen M., 2

Sapir, Edward, 145
Sapir-Whorf hypothesis, 128–29
semantic differential, 89–90
semantic knowledge, 61–62, 89–96
semantic properties, 91–94, 96
sentence patterns, 28, 64–66, 86
sentences, 11, 28, 39, 42, 46, 49, 54, 61, 63–65, 77–79
Shannon, C. E., 53
short vowels, 8, 111–13, 116
Shuy, Roger W., 121–22
sight words, 19, 106
significance, 8, 53
Smith, Henry L., 24
Soffietti, James B., 20, 29
Southgate, Vera, 27
Spache, George, 54
speech and writing differences, 53, 56–59, 79–81, 96, 125, 137, 147–48
speed reading, 61
standard English, 122
Stewart, William A., 127–28
stress and intonation, 28, 60, 64, 104, 106
Strickland, Ruth G., 57, 147
structural linguistics, 31–34
substandard speech, 122
subvocalization, 20, 58, 61, 134, 136–37
Suci, G. C., 89
suprasegmental phonemes, 28, 60, 64, 104, 106
surface structures, 46–49, 63–65, 66–80, 131, 145
    phonology and, 115–16
syllabaries, 98–99
syllabication, 9
syllables, 9, 10, 11, 98–99
systematic phonology, 114, 145

Tannenbaum, P. H., 89

transformations, 46–49, 67–74
Traver, Aileen A., 87

ungrammaticalness, 50, 64, 75, 77–78
universal grammar, 36

Venezky, Richard L., 110–13
vowel(s):
 alternations, 110, 112–14, 145

in English, 7–8, 103–04, 111, 112
reduction, 107
Vygotsky, L. S., 129–30

Wales, R. J., 50
Wardhaugh, Ronald, 9
Weaver, W., 53
word calling, 28, 125, 128, 134
words, 11, 18, 22–23, 28, 32, 83–85, 88–90, 97–99

A 9
B 0
C 1
D 2
E 3
F 4
G 5
H 6
I 7
J 8